Fodor's®

New FIRST EDITION

Pocket
Honolulu &
Waikīkī

D0754275

CONCORDIA UNIVERSITY LIBRARY
PORTLAND, OR 97211

Reprinted from *Fodor's Hawai'i*

Fodor's Travel Publications, Inc.
New York • Toronto • London • Sydney • Auckland
www.fodors.com

Fodor's Pocket Honolulu & Waikīkī

EDITORS: Anastasia Redmond Mills, Audra Epstein

Editorial Contributors: Rob Andrews, David Brown, Heidi Sarna, Helayne Schiff, M. T. Schwartzman (Essential Information editor), Marty Wentzel

Editorial Production: Nicole Revere

Maps: David Lindroth, *cartographer*; Steven K. Amsterdam, *map editor*

Design: Fabrizio La Rocca, *creative director*; Guido Caroti, *associate art director*; Lyndell Brookhouse-Gil, *cover design;* Jolie Novak, *photo editor*

Production/Manufacturing: Mike Costa

Cover Photograph: Douglas Peebles

Copyright

Copyright © 1998 by Fodor's Travel Publications, Inc.

Fodor's is a registered trademark of Fodor's Travel Publications, Inc.

All rights reserved under International and Pan-American Copyright Conventions. Published in the United States by Fodor's Travel Publications, Inc., a subsidiary of Random House, Inc., New York, and simultaneously in Canada by Random House of Canada Limited, Toronto. Distributed by Random House, Inc., New York.

No maps, illustrations, or other portions of this book may be reproduced in any form without written permission from the publisher.

ISBN 0–679–00238–3

Special Sales

Fodor's Travel Publications are available at special discounts for bulk purchases for sales promotions or premiums. Special editions, including personalized covers, excerpts of existing guides, and corporate imprints, can be created in large quantities for special needs. For more information, contact your local bookseller or write to Special Markets, Fodor's Travel Publications, 201 East 50th Street, New York, NY 10022. Inquiries from Canada should be directed to your local Canadian bookseller or sent to Random House of Canada, Ltd., Marketing Department, 2775 Matheson Boulevard East, Mississauga, Ontario L4W 4P7. Inquiries from the United Kingdom should be sent to Fodor's Travel Publications, 20 Vauxhall Bridge Road, London SW1V 2SA, England.

PRINTED IN THE UNITED STATES OF AMERICA

10 9 8 7 6 5 4 3 2 1

CONTENTS

Maps

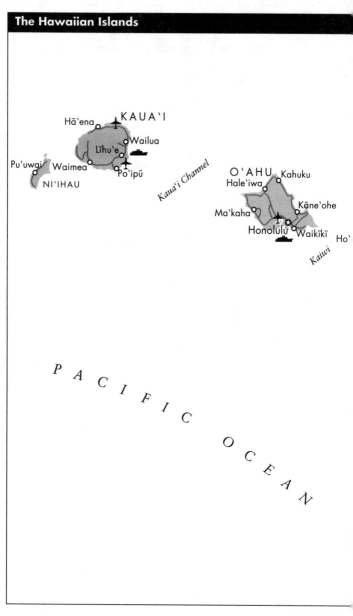

The Hawaiian Islands

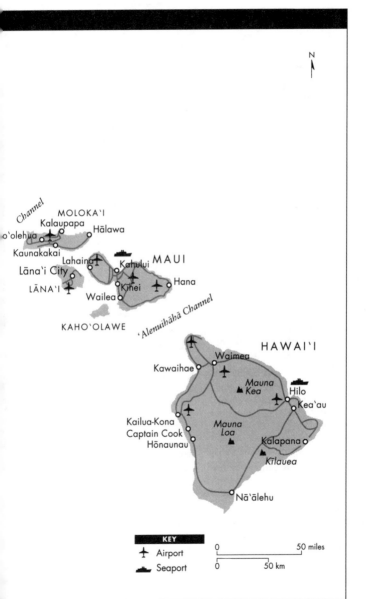

N

MOLOKA'I
Kalaupapa
o'olehua Hālawa
Kaunakakai
Lahaina Kahului MAUI
Lāna'i City Kīhei Hana
LĀNA'I
Wailea
KAHO'OLAWE 'Alenuihāhā Channel
Channel

HAWAI'I
Waimea
Kawaihae
Mauna
Kea Hilo
Kea'au
Kailua-Kona Mauna
Captain Cook Loa
Hōnaunau Kalapana
Kīlauea
Nā'ālehu

KEY		
✈ Airport	0	50 miles
⛴ Seaport	0	50 km

ON THE ROAD WITH FODOR'S

WHEN I PLAN A VA-CATION, the first thing I do is cast around among my friends and colleagues to find someone who's just been where I'm going. That's because there's no substitute for a recommendation from a good friend who knows your tastes, your budget, and your circumstances, someone who's just been there. Unfortunately, such friends are few and far between. So it's nice to know that there's Fodor's *Pocket Honolulu and Waikiki.*

In the first place, this book won't stay home when you hit the road. It will accompany you every step of the way, steering you away from wrong turns and wrong choices and never expecting a thing in return. Most important of all, it's written and assiduously updated by the kind of people you *would* hit up for travel tips if you knew them. They're as choosy as your pickiest friend, except they've probably seen a lot more of Honolulu. In these pages, they don't send you chasing down every town and sight in the Islands but have instead selected the best ones, the ones that are worthy of your time and money.

About Our Writer

Our success in helping to make your trip the best of all possible vacations is a credit to the hard work of our extraordinary writers.

A 17-year resident of Honolulu, **Marty Wentzel** is a prolific freelance writer whose articles have appeared in publications around the world, including *American Way, Modern Bride,* and *ALOHA Magazine.* A specialist in the Hawai'i dining scene, she has coauthored cookbooks with two of the state's top chefs—Sam Choy and Roy Yamaguchi—but she's equally happy eating fresh mango on the beach at sunset.

Connections

We're pleased that the American Society of Travel Agents continues to endorse Fodor's as its guidebook of choice. ASTA is the world's largest and most influential travel trade association, operating in more than 170 countries, with 27,000 members pledged to adhere to a strict code of ethics reflecting the Society's motto, "Integrity in Travel." ASTA shares Fodor's devotion to providing smart, honest travel information and advice to travelers, and we've long recommended that our readers—even those who have guidebooks and traveling friends—consult ASTA member agents for the experience and professionalism they bring to your vacation planning.

On Fodor's Web Site (www.fodors.com), check out the new Resource Center, an on-line companion to the Essential Information section of this book, complete with useful hot links to related sites. In our forums, you can also get lively advice from other travelers and more great tips from Fodor's experts worldwide.

How to Use This Book

Organization

Up front is **Essential Information,** arranged alphabetically by topic. Under each listing you'll find tips and information that will help you accomplish what you need to in Honolulu. You'll also find addresses and telephone numbers of organizations and companies that offer destination-related services and detailed information and publications.

The first chapter in the guide, Destination: Honolulu & Waikīkī, helps get you in the mood for your trip. Pleasures and Pastimes describes the activities and sights that make Honolulu unique, New and Noteworthy cues you in on trends and happenings.

Chapter 2 is subdivided by neighborhood; each subsection recommends a walking or driving tour and lists sights alphabetically. The remaining chapters are arranged in alphabetical order by subject.

Icons and Symbols

★ Our special recommendations
✕ Restaurant
🏨 Lodging establishment
🐤 Good for kids (rubber duck)
☞ Sends you to another section of the guide for more information
✉ Address
☏ Telephone number
☉ Opening and closing times
💲 Admission prices (those we give apply to adults; substantially reduced fees are almost always available for children, students, and senior citizens)

Numbers in white and black circles ③ ❸ that appear on the maps, in the margins, and within the tours correspond to one another.

Hotel Facilities

We always list the facilities that are available—but we don't specify whether you'll be charged extra to use them: When pricing accommodations, always ask what's included. Assume that all rooms have private baths unless noted otherwise. In addition, when you book a room, be sure to mention if you have a disability or are traveling with children, if you prefer a private bath or a certain type of bed, or if you have specific dietary needs or other concerns. The prevalent word lānai indicates a usually covered outdoor area that may be private or part of a public walkway.

Assume that hotels operate on the **European Plan** (EP, with no meals) unless we specify that they use the **Continental Plan** (CP, with a Continental breakfast daily), **Modified American Plan** (MAP, with breakfast and dinner daily), or the **Full American Plan** (FAP, with all meals). A full breakfast includes a hot entrée.

Restaurant Reservations and Dress Codes

Reservations are always a good idea; we mention them only when they're essential or are not accepted. Book as far ahead as you can, and reconfirm as soon as you arrive. Unless otherwise noted, the restaurants listed are open daily for lunch and dinner. We mention dress only when men are required to wear a jacket or a jacket and tie.

Credit Cards

The following abbreviations are used: **AE,** American Express; **D,** Discover; **DC,** Diners Club; **MC,** MasterCard; and **V,** Visa.

Don't Forget to Write

You can use this book in the confidence that all prices and opening times are based on information supplied to us at press time; Fodor's cannot accept responsibility for any errors. Time inevitably brings changes, so always confirm information when it matters—especially if you're making a detour to visit a specific place.

Keeping a travel guide fresh and up-to-date is a big job, and we welcome your feedback, positive *and* negative. If you have complaints, we'll look into them and revise our entries when the facts warrant it. If you've discovered a special place that we haven't included, we'll pass the information along to our correspondents and have them check it out. So send us your thoughts via e-mail at editors@fodors.com (specifying the name of the book on the subject line) or on paper in care of the Hawai'i editor at Fodor's, 201 East 50th Street, New York, New York 10022. In the meantime, have a wonderful trip!

Karen Cure

Karen Cure
Editorial Director

ESSENTIAL INFORMATION

Basic Information on Traveling in Hawai'i, Savvy Tips to Make Your Trip a Breeze, and Companies and Organizations to Contact

AIR TRAVEL

BOOKING YOUR FLIGHT

When you book, **look for nonstop flights** and **remember that "direct" flights stop at least once.** Try to **avoid connecting flights,** which require a change of plane. Two airlines may jointly operate a connecting flight, so ask if your airline operates every segment—you may find that your preferred carrier flies you only part of the way.

CARRIERS

➤ MAJOR AIRLINES: **American** (☎ 800/433–7300) to Honolulu, Maui. **Continental** (☎ 800/525–0280) to Honolulu, Kaua'i. **Delta** (☎ 800/221–1212) to Honolulu, Maui. **Northwest** (☎ 800/225–2525) to Honolulu. **TWA** (☎ 800/221–2000) to Honolulu. **United** (☎ 800/241–6522) to Honolulu, Maui, Big Island, Kaua'i.

➤ SMALLER AIRLINES: **Hawaiian Airlines** (☎ 800/367–5320) to Honolulu and connecting flights to Neighbor Islands.

➤ FROM THE U.K.: **Air New Zealand** (☎ 0181/741–2299). **American** (☎ 0345/789–789). **Continental** (☎ 0800/776–464). **Delta** (☎ 0800/414–767). **United**

(☎ 0800/888–555). All flights require a change of planes on the West Coast. **Trailfinders** (✉ 42–50 Earls Court Rd., Kensington, London, W8 6FT, ☎ 0171/937–5400) can arrange bargain flights.

CHECK IN & BOARDING

The first to get bumped off planes are passengers who checked in late and those flying on discounted tickets, so **get to the gate and check in as early as possible,** especially during peak periods.

Although the trend on international flights is to drop reconfirmation requirements, many airlines still ask you to reconfirm each leg of your international itinerary. Failure to do so may result in your reservation being canceled.

Always **bring a government-issued photo ID to the airport.** You may be asked to show it before you are allowed to check in.

CUTTING COSTS

It's smart to **call a number of airlines, and when you are quoted a good price, reserve it or book it on the spot**—the same fare may not be available the next day. Most low-fare tickets are nonrefundable. To get the lowest airfare, **check different routings.** Compare prices of flights to and from different airports if your destination or home city has more than one gateway. Also price off-peak flights, which may be significantly less expensive. If you're traveling a great distance, try pricing two round-trip tickets, say New York–LA and LA–Honolulu.

When flying within the U.S., **plan to stay over a Saturday night** and **travel during the middle of the week** to get the lowest fare. These low fares are usually priced for round-trip travel and are nonrefundable. You can, however, change your return date for a fee ($75 on most major airlines).

Travel agents, especially those who specialize in finding the lowest fares (☞ Discounts & Deals, *below*), can be especially helpful when booking a plane ticket. When you're quoted a price, **ask your agent if the price is likely to get any lower.** Good agents know the seasonal fluctuations of airfares and can usually anticipate a sale or fare war. However, waiting can be risky: The fare could go *up* as seats become scarce, and you may wait so long that your preferred flight sells out.

Charter flights are the least expensive and the least reliable—with chronically late departures and occasional cancellations. They also tend to depart less frequently (usu-ally once a week) than do regularly scheduled flights. Nevertheless, the savings are often worth the potential annoyance.

➤ CHARTER FLIGHTS: **American Trans Air** (☎ 800/225–9920) and **Hawaiian Airlines** (☎ 808/838–1555 or 800/367–5320).

FLYING TIMES

Flying time to Honolulu is about 10 hours from New York, 6 hours from Chicago, and 3 hours from Los Angeles.

HOW TO COMPLAIN

If your baggage goes astray or your flight goes awry, complain right away. Most carriers require that you **file a claim immediately.**

AIRPORTS

Hawai'i's major gateway, **Honolulu International Airport,** is about a five-hour flight from West Coast cities and a 20-minute drive from Waikīkī.

➤ AIRPORT INFORMATION: **Honolulu International** (☎ 808/836–6413).

BETWEEN THE AIRPORT AND WAIKĪKĪ

There are taxis right at the airport baggage claim exit. At $1.50 start-up plus $1.50 for each mile, the fare to Waikīkī will run approximately $20, plus tip. Drivers are also allowed to charge 30¢ per suitcase. TransHawaiian Services runs an airport shuttle service to Waikīkī ($8 one-way, $14 round-trip). The municipal bus is only $1, but you are allowed only one bag that must fit on your lap. Some hotels have their own pickup service. Check when you book your reservations.

➤ AIRPORT SHUTTLE: **TransHawaiian Services** (☎ 808/566–7333).

BUS TRAVEL

You can go all around the island or just down Kalākaua Avenue for $1 on Honolulu's municipal transportation system, affectionately known as The Bus. You are also entitled to one free transfer per fare if you ask for it when boarding. Board at the front of the bus. Exact change is required, and dollar bills are accepted. A four-day pass costs $10 and is sold at the more than 30 ABC Stores (Hawaiian chain stores that sell sundries and are geared to tourists) in Waikīkī. Monthly passes cost $25.

There are no official bus-route maps, but you can find privately published booklets at most drugstores and other convenience outlets. The important route numbers for Waikīkī are 2, 4, 8, 19, 20, and 58. If you venture afield, you can always get back on one of these.

There are also a number of brightly painted private buses, many free, that will take you to such commercial attractions as dinner cruises, garment factories, and the like.

➤ BUS INFORMATION: **The Bus** (☎ 808/848–5555).

CAR RENTAL

Rates in Honolulu begin at $28 a day and $144 a week for an economy car with air-conditioning, an automatic transmission, and with unlimited mileage. This does not include tax on car rentals, which is 4.16%, or a $2-per-day road tax. During peak seasons—summer, Christmas vacations, and February—car-rental reservations are necessary.

➤ MAJOR AGENCIES: **Alamo** (☎ 800/327–9633, 0800/272–2000 in the U.K.). **Avis** (☎ 800/331–1212, 800/879–2847 in Canada, 008/225–533 in Australia). **Budget** (☎ 800/527–0700, 0800/181181 in the U.K.). **Dollar** (☎ 800/800–4000; 0990/565656 in the U.K., where it is known as Eurodollar). **Hertz** (☎ 800/654–3131, 800/263–0600 in Canada, 0345/555888 in the U.K., 03/9222–2523 in Australia, 03/358–6777 in New Zealand). **National InterRent** (☎ 800/227–7368; 0345/222525 in the U.K., where it is known as Europcar InterRent).

➤ LOCAL AGENCIES: **Classic Car Rentals** (☎ 808/923–6446). **Courtesy Car and Truck Rentals** (☎ 808/831–2277). **Thrifty Car Rental** (☎ 808/973–5188). **VIP Car Rentals** (☎ 808/922–4605).

CUTTING COSTS

To get the best deal, **book through a travel agent who is**

willing to shop around. When pricing cars, **ask about the location of the rental lot.** Some off-airport locations offer lower rates, and their lots are only minutes from the terminal via complimentary shuttle. You also may want to **price local car-rental companies,** whose rates may be lower still, although their service and maintenance may not be as good as those of a name-brand agency. Remember to ask about required deposits and cancellation penalties.

Also **ask your travel agent about a company's customer-service record.** How has the company responded to late plane arrivals and vehicle mishaps? Are there often lines at the rental counter? If you're traveling during a holiday period, does a confirmed reservation guarantee you a car?

Be sure to **look into wholesalers,** companies that do not own fleets but rent in bulk from those that do and often offer better rates than traditional car-rental operations. Prices are best during off-peak periods.

➤ RENTAL WHOLESALERS: **Auto Europe** (☎ 207/842–2000 or 800/223–5555, ℻ 800/235–6321). **Kemwel Holiday Autos** (☎ 914/835–5555 or 800/678–0678, ℻ 914/835–5126).

INSURANCE

When driving a rented car you are generally responsible for any damage to or loss of the vehicle. You also are liable for any property damage or personal injury that you may cause while driving. Before you rent, **see what coverage you already have** under the terms of your personal auto-insurance policy and credit cards.

For about $15 to $20 per day, rental companies sell protection, known as a collision- or loss-damage waiver (CDW or LDW), that eliminates your liability for damage to the car; it's always optional and should never be automatically added to your bill.

In most states you don't need a CDW if you have personal auto insurance or other liability insurance. However, **make sure you have enough coverage to pay for the car.** If you do not have auto insurance or an umbrella policy that covers damage to third parties, purchasing liability insurance and a CDW or LDW is highly recommended.

REQUIREMENTS

In Hawai'i you must be 21 to rent a car, and rates may be higher if you're under 25. You'll pay extra for child seats (about $3 per day), which are compulsory for children under five, and for additional drivers (about $2 per day). Non-U.S. residents will need a reservation voucher, a passport, a driver's license, and a travel policy that covers each driver, in order to pick up a car.

CAR TRAVEL

Be sure to **buckle up.** Hawai'i has a strictly enforced seat-belt law for front-seat passengers. Children under three must be in a car seat (available from car-rental agencies). The highway speed limit is usually 55 mph; in-town traffic moves from 25 to 40 mph. Jaywalking is very common, so be particularly watchful for pedestrians, especially in congested areas such as Waikīkī. Unauthorized use of a parking space reserved for persons with disabilities can net you a $150 fine.

It's difficult to get lost in most of Hawai'i. Roads and streets, although they may challenge the visitor's tongue (Kalaniana'ole Highway, for example), are well marked. Keep an eye open for the Hawai'i Visitors and Convention Bureau's red-caped warrior signs that mark major visitor attractions and scenic spots. Ask for a map at the car-rental counter; free visitor publications containing good-quality maps can be found on all islands, too. Although it's hard to get lost, driving in Honolulu can be frustrating, as many streets are one-way and there are many traffic lights.

Asking for directions will almost always produce a helpful explanation from the locals, but you should be prepared for an island term or two. Instead of using compass directions, Hawai'i residents refer to places as being either *mauka* (toward the mountains) or *makai* (toward the ocean) from one another. Other directions depend on your location: In Honolulu, for example, people say to "go Diamond Head," which means toward the famous landmark, or to "go *'ewa,*" meaning the opposite direction. A shop on the mauka-Diamond Head corner of a street is on the mountain side of the street on the corner closest to Diamond Head. It all makes perfect sense once you get the lay of the land.

CONSUMER PROTECTION

Whenever possible, **pay with a major credit card** so you can cancel payment or get reimbursed if there's a problem, provided that you can provide documentation. This is the best way to pay, whether you're buying travel arrangements before your trip or shopping at your destination.

If you're doing business with a particular company for the first time, **contact your local Better Business Bureau and the attorney general's offices** in your state and the company's home state, as well. Have any complaints been filed?

Finally, if you're buying a package or tour, always **consider travel insurance** that includes default coverage (☞ Insurance, *below*).

➤ LOCAL BBBs: Council of Better Business Bureaus (✉ 4200 Wilson Blvd., Suite 800, Arlington, VA 22203, ☎ 703/276–0100, 🖷 703/525–8277).

CUSTOMS & DUTIES

IN HAWAIʻI

Plants and plant products are subject to regulation by the Department of Agriculture, both on entering and leaving Hawaiʻi. Pineapples and coconuts with the packer's agricultural inspection stamp pass freely; papayas must be treated, inspected, and stamped. All other fruits are banned for export to the U.S. mainland. Flowers pass except for gardenia, rose leaves, jade vine, and mauna loa. Also banned are insects, snails, soil, coffee, cotton, cacti, sugarcane, and all berry plants.

Leave dogs and other pets at home. A strict 30-day quarantine is imposed to keep out rabies, which is nonexistent in Hawaiʻi.

IN AUSTRALIA

Australia residents who are 18 or older may bring back $A400 worth of souvenirs and gifts (including jewelry), 250 cigarettes or 250 grams of tobacco, and 1,125 ml of alcohol (including wine, beer, and spirits). Residents under 18 may bring back $A200 worth of goods.

➤ INFORMATION: **Australian Customs Service** (Regional Director, ✉ Box 8, Sydney, NSW 2001,

☎ 02/9213–2000, 🖷 02/9213–4000).

IN CANADA

Canadian residents who have been out of Canada for at least seven days may bring in C$500 worth of goods duty-free. If you've been away less than seven days but more than 48 hours, the duty-free allowance drops to C$200; if your trip lasts 24–48 hours, the allowance is C$50. You may not pool allowances with family members. Goods claimed under the C$500 exemption may follow you by mail; those claimed under the lesser exemptions must accompany you. Alcohol and tobacco products may be included in the seven-day and 48-hour exemptions but not in the 24-hour exemption. If you meet the age requirements of the province or territory through which you reenter Canada, you may bring in, duty-free, 1.14 liters (40 imperial ounces) of wine or liquor *or* 24 12-ounce cans or bottles of beer or ale. If you are 16 or older you may bring in, duty-free, 200 cigarettes and 50 cigars.

You may send an unlimited number of gifts worth up to C$60 each duty-free to Canada. Label the package UNSOLICITED GIFT—VALUE UNDER $60. Alcohol and tobacco are excluded.

➤ INFORMATION: **Revenue Canada** (✉ 2265 St. Laurent Blvd. S, Ot-

tawa, Ontario K1G 4K3, ☎ 613/
993–0534, 800/461–9999 in
Canada).

IN NEW ZEALAND

If you're 17 or older, you may
bring back $700 worth of sou-
venirs and gifts. Your duty-free allowance also includes 4.5 liters of
wine or beer; one 1,125-ml bottle
of spirits; and either 200
cigarettes, 250 grams of tobacco,
50 cigars, or a combo of all three
up to 250 grams.

➤ INFORMATION: **New Zealand
Customs** (⊠ Custom House, ⊠
50 Anzac Ave., Box 29, Auckland,
New Zealand, ☎ 09/359–6655,
☎ 09/309–2978).

IN THE U.K.

From countries outside the EU, including the United States, you may
import, duty-free, 200 cigarettes
or 50 cigars; 1 liter of spirits or 2
liters of fortified or sparkling wine
or liqueurs; 2 liters of still table
wine; 60 milliliters of perfume;
250 milliliters of toilet water; plus
£136 worth of other goods, including gifts and souvenirs.

➤ INFORMATION: **HM Customs
and Excise** (⊠ Dorset House, ⊠
Stamford St., London SE1 9NG,
☎ 0171/202–4227).

IN THE U.S.

Non-U.S. residents ages 21 and
older may import into the United
States 200 cigarettes or 50 cigars
or 2 kilograms of tobacco, 1 liter
of alcohol, and gifts worth $100.

Prohibited items include meat
products, seeds, plants, and fruits.

➤ INFORMATION: **U.S. Customs
Service** (Inquiries, ⊠ Box 7407,
Washington, DC 20044, ☎ 202/
927–6724; complaints, Office of
Regulations and Rulings, ⊠ 1301
Constitution Ave. NW, Washington, DC 20229; registration of
equipment, Resource Manage-
ment, ⊠ 1301 Constitution Ave.
NW, Washington DC 20229, ☎
202/927–0540).

DISCOUNTS & DEALS

DISCOUNT RESERVATIONS

To save money, **look into discount-
reservations services** with toll-free
numbers, which use their buying
power to get a better price on hotels, airline tickets, even car
rentals. When booking a room, always **call the hotel's local toll-free
number** (if one is available) rather
than the central reservations number—you'll often get a better
price. Always ask about special
packages or corporate rates.

➤ AIRLINE TICKETS: ☎ **800/FLY–
4–LESS.** ☎ **800/FLY–ASAP.**

➤ HOTEL ROOMS: **Players Express
Vacations** (☎ 800/458–6161).
RMC Travel (☎ 800/245–5738).
Steigenberger Reservation Service
(☎ 800/223–5652).

HEALTH

From 1996 to 1998, reported
cases of leptospirosis, a tropical
disease spread by animal urine

and carried in freshwater streams and mud, were up 100% in Hawai'i, although the disease is still rare—there were only 60 cases reported in 1997. Initial symptoms include headaches, fever, nausea, and red eyes; if left untreated it can cause liver and kidney damage, respiratory failure, internal bleeding, and death.

DIVERS' ALERT
Do not fly within 24 hours after scuba diving.

MEDICAL ASSISTANCE
At Doctors on Call a doctor, laboratory/radiology technician, and nurses are always on duty. Appointments are recommended but not necessary. Dozens of kinds of medical insurance are accepted, including Medicare, Medicaid, and most kinds of travel insurance. Doctors Who Care offers quick service for such minor ailments as sunburn.

➤ DOCTORS: **Doctors on Call** (⊠ Bank of Hawai'i Bldg., 2222 Kalākaua Ave., 2nd floor, ☎ 808/971–6000. **Doctors Who Care** (⊠ Pacific Beach Hotel, 2490 Kalākaua Ave., ☎ 808/926–7776)

➤ EMERGENCIES: **Police, fire department, ambulance,** and **suicide center** (☎ 911). **Coast Guard Rescue** (☎ 800/552–6458).

➤ HOSPITALS: **Castle Medical Center** (⊠ 640 Ulukahiki, Kailua, ☎ 808/263–5500). **Kapiolani Medical Center for Women and Chil-** dren (⊠ 1319 Punahou St., Honolulu, ☎ 808/973–8511). **Queen's Medical Center** (⊠ 1301 Punchbowl St., Honolulu, ☎ 808/538–9011). **Straub Clinic** (⊠ 888 S. King St., Honolulu, ☎ 808/522–4000).

➤ LATE-NIGHT PHARMACIES: **Kuhio Pharmacy** (⊠ Outrigger West Hotel, 2330 Kuhio Ave., ☎ 808/923–4466). **Long's Drugs Store** (⊠ Ala Moana Shopping Center, 1450 Ala Moana Blvd., 2nd level, ☎ 808/949–4010).

INSURANCE
Travel insurance is the best way to **protect yourself against financial loss.** The most useful plan is a comprehensive policy that includes coverage for trip cancellation and interruption, default, trip delay, and medical expenses (with a waiver for preexisting conditions).

Without insurance, you will lose all or most of your money if you cancel your trip, regardless of the reason. Default insurance covers you if your tour operator, airline, or cruise line goes out of business. Trip-delay covers unforeseen expenses that you may incur due to bad weather or mechanical delays. It's important to compare the fine print regarding trip-delay coverage when comparing policies.

For overseas travel, one of the most important components of travel insurance is its medical coverage. Supplemental health insurance will pick up the cost of your medical bills should you get sick or injured while traveling. Residents of the United Kingdom can buy an annual travel-insurance policy valid for most vacations taken during the year in which the coverage is purchased. If you are pregnant or have a preexisting condition, make sure you're covered. British citizens should buy extra medical coverage when traveling overseas, according to the Association of British Insurers. Australian travelers should buy travel insurance, including extra medical coverage, whenever they go abroad, according to the Insurance Council of Australia.

Always **buy travel insurance directly from the insurance company**; if you buy it from a cruise line, airline, or tour operator that goes out of business you probably will not be covered for the agency or operator's default, a major risk. Before you make any purchase, **review your existing health and home-owner's policies** to find out whether they cover expenses incurred while traveling.

➤ TRAVEL INSURERS: In the U.S., **Access America** (⊠ 6600 W. Broad St., Richmond, VA 23230, ☎ 804/285–3300 or 800/284–8300). **Travel Guard International** (⊠ 1145 Clark St., Stevens Point, WI 54481, ☎ 715/345–0505 or 800/826–1300). In Canada, **Mutual of Omaha** (⊠ Travel Division, ⊠ 500 University Ave.,

Toronto, Ontario M5G 1V8, ☎ 416/598–4083, 800/268–8825 in Canada).

➤ INSURANCE INFORMATION: In the U.K., **Association of British Insurers** (⊠ 51 Gresham St., London EC2V 7HQ, ☎ 0171/600–3333). In Australia, the **Insurance Council of Australia** (☎ 613/9614–1077, FAX 613/9614–7924).

LODGING

APARTMENT & VILLA RENTALS

If you want a home base that's roomy enough for a family and comes with cooking facilities, **consider a furnished rental.** These can save you money, especially if you're traveling with a large group of people. Home-exchange directories list rentals (often second homes owned by prospective house swappers), and some services search for a house or apartment for you and handle the paperwork. Up-front registration fees may apply.

➤ RENTAL AGENTS: **Europa-Let/Tropical Inn-Let** (⊠ 92 N. Main St., Ashland, OR 97520, ☎ 541/482–5806 or 800/462–4486, FAX 541/482–0660). **Hideaways International** (⊠ 767 Islington St., Portsmouth, NH 03801, ☎ 603/430–4433 or 800/843–4433, FAX 603/430–4444; membership $99) is a club for travelers who arrange rentals among themselves. **Property Rentals International** (⊠ 1008 Mansfield Crossing Rd., Richmond, VA 23236, ☎ 804/

378–6054 or 800/220–3332, FAX 804/379–2073). **RDI World** (⊠ Box 329, Wayne, PA 19087, ☎ 610/353–2335, FAX 610/353–7756) lists properties that can be rented directly from their owners. **Rent-a-Home International** (⊠ 7200 34th Ave. NW, Seattle, WA 98117, ☎ 206/789–9377 or 800/488–7368, FAX 206/789–9379). **Vacation Home Rentals Worldwide** (⊠ 235 Kensington Ave., Norwood, NJ 07648, ☎ 201/767–9393 or 800/633–3284, FAX 201/767–5510).

B&BS

➤ RESERVATION SERVICES: **Pacific Hawai'i Bed and Breakfast** (⊠ 99-1661 Aiea Heights Dr., Aiea, O'ahu, HI 96701, ☎ 808/486–8838, 800/262–6026, or 800/999–6026), **Bed and Breakfast Honolulu** (statewide) (⊠ 3242 Kaohinani Dr., Honolulu, HI 96817, ☎ 808/595–3298, or 800/288–4666, FAX 808/595–2030), **Volcano Reservations–Select Statewide Accommodations** (⊠ Box 998, Volcano Village, Hawai'i 96785, ☎ 808/967–7244, or 800/736–7140, FAX 808/967-8660), and **Hawai'i's Best Bed and Breakfasts** (⊠ Box 563, Kamuela, Hawai'i 96743, ☎ 808/885–4550 or 800/262–9912, FAX 808/885–0559), which specializes in upscale properties.

MOPEDS, MOTORCYCLES, AND BICYCLES

Aloha Funway Rentals rents a variety of motorcycles for $50–$200 a day. Blue Sky Rentals & Sports Center rents mopeds for $20 a day (8–6) and $25 for 24 hours. Mountain bikes cost $15 a day and $20 for 24 hours plus a $25 deposit, including helmet, lock, and water bottle.

➤ RENTAL AGENCIES: **Aloha Funway Rentals** (☎ 808/973–5188). **Blue Sky Rentals & Sports Center** (☎ 808/947–0101).

PACKING

PACKING LIST

Hawai'i is casual: Sandals, bathing suits, and comfortable, informal clothing are the norm. In summer synthetic slacks and shirts, although easy to care for, can be uncomfortably warm. If you need a bathing cap, bring it with you: You can waste hours searching for one. All major hotels in Hawai'i provide beach towels.

Bring sunscreen. This is the tropics, and the ultraviolet rays are powerful. Don't forget to **reapply sunscreen periodically during the day,** since perspiration can wash it away. There are many tanning oils on the market in Hawai'i, including coconut and *kukui* (the nut from a local tree) oils, but doctors warn that they will sauté your skin.

As for clothing, in the Hawaiian Islands there's a saying that when a man wears a suit during the day, he's either going for a loan or he's a lawyer trying a case. Only a few upscale restaurants require a jacket for dinner, and none require a tie. The aloha shirt is accepted dress in Hawai'i for business and most social occasions. Shorts are acceptable daytime attire, along with a T-shirt or polo shirt. Golfers should remember that many courses have dress codes requiring a collared shirt. If you're not prepared, you can pick up appropriate clothing at resort pro shops. If you're visiting in winter or planning to visit a volcano area, bring a sweater or light- to medium-weight jacket. Trade winds cool things off when the sun goes down, and things get chilly above 10,000 ft.

If you're a woman and don't own a *pareo,* buy one in Hawai'i. It's simply a length of light cotton (about 1½–2 yds long), usually in a tropical motif, that can be worn as a beach wrap, a skirt, or a dozen other wrap-up fashions. A pareo is useful wherever you go, regardless of the climate. It makes a good bathrobe, so you don't have to pack one. You can even tie it up as a handbag or sit on it at the beach.

PASSPORTS

PASSPORT OFFICES
The best time to apply for a passport or to renew is during the fall and winter. Before any trip, be sure to check your passport's expiration date and, if necessary, renew it as soon as possible.

➤ AUSTRALIAN CITIZENS: **Australian Passport Office** (☎ 131–232).

➤ NEW ZEALAND CITIZENS: **New Zealand Passport Office** (☎ 04/494–0700 for information on how to apply, 0800/727–776 for information on applications already submitted).

➤ U.K. CITIZENS: **London Passport Office** (☎ 0990/21010 for fees and documentation requirements and to request an emergency passport).

SIGHTSEEING TOURS

➤ EXCURSIONS: **Little Circle Tour** covers the territory discussed in The East O'ahu Ring (☞ Chapter 2). Tours last a half day and cost between $25 and $40. **Pearl Harbor and City** tours include the boat tour to Pearl Harbor run by the National Park Service. Tours cost between $25 and $40.

➤ SEA TOURS: **Dream Cruises** (✉ 1085 Ala Moana Blvd., Suite 103, Honolulu 96814, ☎ 808/592–5200) presents tours of Pearl Harbor aboard the 100-ft motor yacht *American Dream*. The trip takes place in the early morning to coincide with the time that Pearl Harbor was attacked on Dec. 7, 1941. It includes a stop near the USS *Arizona* Memorial, where the captain conducts a brief memorial service and lei placement ceremony. Narration and videos help describe the sights. In winter, this cruise is paired with a whale watch. Tours are run daily between 7:30 AM and 10:15 AM and cost $19.95.

TOUR COMPANIES

Many ground tour companies handle these excursions. Some herd you onto an air-conditioned bus and others use smaller vans. Vans are recommended because less time is spent picking up passengers, and you get to know your fellow passengers and your tour guide. Whether you go by bus or van, you'll probably be touring in top-of-the-line equipment, as the competition among these companies is fierce, and everyone has to keep up. If you're booking through your hotel travel desk, ask whether you'll be on a bus or a van and exactly what the tour includes in the way of actual "get-off-the-bus" stops and "window sights."

Most of the tour guides have been in the business for years. Many have taken special Hawaiiana classes to learn their history and lore. Tipping ($2 per person at least) is customary. **American Express** (☎ 808/947–2607) books through several tour companies and can help you choose which tour best suits your needs. **E Noa Tours** (☎ 808/591–2561) uses minibuses exclusively and likes to get you into the great outdoors. **Polynesian Adventure Tours** (☎ 808/833–3000) has motorcoaches, vans, and minicoaches. **Polynesian Hospitality** (☎ 808/593–9890) provides narrated tours. **Roberts Hawai'i** (☎ 808/539–9400) has equipment ranging from vans to presidential limousines. **Trans Hawaiian Services** (☎ 808/566–7000) offers multilingual tours.

➤ UNDERWATER TOURS: *Atlantis Submarines* (✉ 1600 Kapi'olani Blvd., Suite 1630, Honolulu 96814, ☎ 808/973–9811) operates two vessels off Waikīkī: a 65-ft, 80-ton sub carrying up to 48 passengers, and a newer 102-ft, 64-passenger craft. Rides are popular with the children; a trip includes a catamaran ride to the dive site, providing great views of the Waikīkī and Diamond Head shoreline. The subs dive up to 100 ft to see a sunken Navy yard oiler and an artificial reef populated by brilliant fish. While the human-made concrete reef looks more like a fish tenement, it is drawing reef fish back to the area. You get a two-hour cruise with informative narration. The dive itself lasts about one hour. Children must be at least 3 ft tall to board. Note: Flash photography will not work; use film speed ASA 200 or above without flash. Tours cost $89–$105, depending on which sub (48- or 64-ft) you go on.

➤ WALKING TOURS: **Aunty Malia's Walking Tours** (✉ Hyatt Regency Waikīkī, 2424 Kalākaua Ave., ☎ 808/923–1234) are led by Aunty Malia, the Hyatt Regency's resident Hawaiiana expert. Free three-hour strolls through the streets of Waikīkī take in all the historic and cultural sites of interest along the way. Tours begin and end at the hotel. There is a minimum of six people per tour, and reservations are required. Tours begin daily at 10 throughout summer, weather permitting.

Chinatown Walking Tour ☎ 808/ 533–3181 offers a fascinating peek into herbal shops, an acupuncturist's office, open-air markets, and specialty stores. The 2½-hour tour is sponsored by the Chinese Chamber of Commerce. Reservations are required. Tours depart from the Chinese Chamber of Commerce (✉ 42 N. King St.) on Tuesday at 9:30. The cost is $5.

Historic Downtown Walking Tours (☎ 808/531–0481) are led b volunteers from the Mission Houses Museum (✉ 553 S. King St.). Guides take you on a two-hour walk through Honolulu, where historic sites stand side by side with modern business towers. During the first hour, you get a tour of the Mission Houses themselves. Reservations are required. Tours are run between 9:30 AM and 12:30 PM on Thursdays and cost $7.

Honolulu Time Walks (☎ 808/ 943–0371) are fun jaunts led by appropriately costumed narrators. Tours include "Haunted Honolulu," "Honolulu's Crime Beat," "Mysteries of Mōʻiliʻili," "Mark Twain's Honolulu," and the "Old Hawaiʻi Saloon Walk." The company also presents theater shows and films about the Islands. Costs range from $7 to $45.

TAXIS AND LIMOUSINES

You can usually get a taxi right outside your hotel. Most restaurants will call a taxi for you. Rates are $1.50 at the drop of the flag, plus $1.50 per mile. Drivers are generally courteous, and the cars are in good condition, many of them air-conditioned. The two biggest taxicab companies are Charley's, a fleet of company-owned cabs, and SIDA of Hawaiʻi, Inc., an association of individually owned cabs. Limousines cost $60 per hour, plus tax and tip.

➤ LIMOUSINE SERVICES: **Cloud Nine Limousine Service** (☎ 808/ 524–7999). **Lowy Limousine Service** (☎ 808/455–2444).

➤ TAXI COMPANIES: **Charley's** (☎ 808/531–1333). **SIDA of Hawaiʻi, Inc.** (☎ 808/836–0011).

TELEPHONES

COUNTRY CODES
The country code for the United States is 1.

DIRECTORY & OPERATOR INFORMATION
Dial 808/555–1212 for directory information and, within the state, 0 for an operator.

LOCAL CALLS
All Hawaiian island telephones have the area code 808; this area code must be used for interisland calls, as well as calls from other area codes. Many toll-free 800 numbers for hotels and other es-

tablishments may not be dialed from within the Islands. For facilities that have both an 808 phone number and an 800 number, use the 808 number once you arrive in Hawai'i. Include the area code when dialing if you are phoning to another island.

LONG-DISTANCE CALLS

Competitive long-distance carriers make calling within the United States relatively convenient and let you avoid hotel surcharges. By dialing an 800 number, you can get connected to the long-distance company of your choice.

➤ LONG-DISTANCE CARRIERS: AT&T (☎ 800/225–5288). MCI (☎ 800/888–8000). Sprint (☎ 800/366–2255).

TOUR OPERATORS

Buying a prepackaged tour or independent vacation can make your trip to Hawai'i less expensive and more hassle-free.

BOOKING WITH AN AGENT

Travel agents are excellent resources. In fact, large operators accept bookings made only through travel agents. But it's a good idea to **collect brochures from several agencies,** because some agents' suggestions may be influenced by relationships with tour and package firms that reward them for volume sales. If you have a special interest, **find an agent with expertise in that area;** ASTA (☞ Travel Agencies, *below*)

has a database of specialists worldwide.

Make sure your travel agent knows the accommodations and other services. Ask about the hotel's location, room size, beds, and whether it has a pool, room service, or programs for children, if you care about these. Has your agent been there in person or sent others you can contact?

Do some homework on your own, too: Local tourism boards can provide information about lesser-known and small-niche operators, some of which may sell only direct.

BUYER BEWARE

Each year consumers are stranded or lose their money when tour operators—even very large ones with excellent reputations—go out of business. So **check out the operator.** Find out how long the company has been in business, and ask several travel agents about its reputation. If the package or tour you are considering is priced lower than in your wildest dreams, **be skeptical.** Try to **book with a company that has a consumer-protection program.** If the operator has such a program, you'll find information about it in the company's brochure. If the operator you are considering does not offer some kind of consumer protection, then ask for references from satisfied customers.

In the U.S., members of the National Tour Association and

United States Tour Operators Association are required to set aside funds to cover your payments and travel arrangements in case the company defaults. It's also a good idea to choose a company that participates in the American Society of Travel Agent's Tour Operator Program (TOP). This gives you a forum if there are any disputes between you and your tour operator; ASTA will act as mediator.

➤ TOUR-OPERATOR RECOMMENDATIONS: **American Society of Travel Agents** (☞ Travel Agencies, *below*). **National Tour Association** (⊠ NTA, ⊠ 546 E. Main St., Lexington, KY 40508, ☎ 606/226–4444 or 800/755–8687). **United States Tour Operators Association** (⊠ USTOA, ⊠ 342 Madison Ave., Suite 1522, New York, NY 10173, ☎ 212/599–6599 or 800/468–7862, ℻ 212/599–6744).

COSTS

Make sure you know exactly what is covered, and **beware of hidden costs.** Are taxes, tips, and service charges included? Transfers and baggage handling? Entertainment and excursions? These can add up.

TRAVEL AGENCIES

A good travel agent puts your needs first. Look for an agency that has been in business at least five years, emphasizes customer service, and has someone on staff who specializes in your destination. In addition, **make sure the agency belongs to a professional trade organization,** such as ASTA in the United States. If your travel agency is also acting as your tour operator, *see* Buyer Beware *in* Tour Operators, *above.*

➤ LOCAL AGENT REFERRALS: **American Society of Travel Agents** (ASTA, ☎ 800/965–2782 24-hr hot line, ℻ 703/684–8319). **Association of British Travel Agents** (⊠ 55–57 Newman St., London W1P 4AH, ☎ 0171/637–2444, ℻ 0171/637–0713). **Association of Canadian Travel Agents** (⊠ Suite 201, 1729 Bank St., Ottawa, Ontario K1V 7Z5, ☎ 613/521–0474, ℻ 613/521–0805). **Australian Federation of Travel Agents** (☎ 02/9264–3299). **Travel Agents' Association of New Zealand** (☎ 04/499–0104).

TROLLEY

An **open trolley** (☎ 808/596–2199) cruises Waikīkī, the Ala Moana area, and downtown, making 20 stops along a two-hour route. The conductor narrates, pointing out sights and shopping, dining, and entertainment opportunities along the way. The trolley departs from the Royal Hawaiian Shopping Center every 15 minutes daily 8–4:30. Buy an all-day pass from the conductor for $18.

VISITOR INFORMATION

TOURIST INFORMATION

Before you go, contact the Hawai'i Visitors & Convention Bureau for general information, an accommodations and car-rental guide (which includes everything from a property's distance from the beach to its amenities), and an entertainment and dining listing containing one-line descriptions of bureau members.

➤ CONTACT: **Hawai'i Visitors & Convention Bureau** (✉ 2270 Kalakaua Ave., Suite 801, Honolulu, HI 96817, ☎ 808/923–1811). For brochures on the Islands call 800/464–2924. In the United Kingdom contact the **Hawai'i Visitors & Convention Bureau** (✉ Box 208, Sunbury, Middlesex, TW16 5RJ, ☎ 0181/941–4009). Send a £2 check or postal order for an information pack.

WEB SITES

Do **check out the World Wide Web when you're planning.** Fodor's Web site, www.fodors.com, is a great place to start. For more information specifically on Honolulu, visit: **www.visit.hawaii.org,** the official Web site of the Hawai'i Convention and Visitors Bureau; **www.hawaiian-index.com;** **www.starbulletin.com,** the site of Honolulu's daily paper, the

Honolulu Star-Bulletin.; **www.hawaii.net;** and **www.search-hawaii.com.**

WHEN TO GO

Hawai'i's long days of sunshine and fairly mild year-round temperatures make it a year-round destination. In resort areas near sea level, the average afternoon temperature during the coldest winter months of December and January is 75°F; during the hottest months of August and September the temperature often reaches 92°F.

Winter is the season when most travelers prefer to head for the islands—from mid-December through mid-April. Room rates average 10%–15% higher during this winter season. The only weather change most areas experience during the December–February span is a few more days of rainfall, though the sun is rarely hidden behind the clouds for a solid 24-hour period.

CLIMATE

The following are average maximum and minimum temperatures for Honolulu.

HONOLULU

Jan.	80F	27C	May	85F	29C	Sept.	88F	31C
	65	18		70	21		73	23
Feb.	80F	27C	June	86F	30C	Oct.	87F	31C
	65	18		72	22		72	22
Mar.	81F	27C	July	87F	31C	Nov.	84F	29C
	69	21		73	23		69	21
Apr.	83F	28C	Aug.	88F	31C	Dec.	81F	27C
	69	21		74	23		67	19

1 Destination: Honolulu & Waikīkī

COMING TO PARADISE

THE FIRST TIME I TRAVELED from California to Hawai'i, I wondered if I would ever touch ground again—the flight seemed endless. Then, 5½ hours and 2,390 mi later, a landscape new to me came into view. I could see the green spires of the Ko'olau Mountains, the glimmering high-rises of Waikīkī, the aqua intensity of the water, the fleets of white sails dotting the sea, and the network of crisscrossing freeways, pineapple plantations, and sugarcane fields.

A trip to Hawai'i from anywhere else in the world makes you aware of its remoteness—it waits in the middle of the Pacific Ocean like a crossroads as well as a cloister. This island group is the most isolated archipelago in the world, more than 2,000 mi from the closest major land mass. The Hawaiian Islands are at the northernmost reaches of Polynesia (meaning "many islands"), within an area referred to as the Polynesian Triangle; New Zealand and Easter Island form the triangle's other points. Yet, while it is influenced by its distant Polynesian, Asian, and American neighbors, Hawai'i remains very much its own destination. As a state, it often seems as exotic as a foreign land.

Visitors often arrive with the sort of dazed, uncertain look that comes from spending hours cooped up inside a jumbo jet. Gradually their quizzical expressions will change to ones of delight, as the scent of tropical flowers carried aloft cool trade winds surrounds them and refreshes their weary lungs and limbs. Within hours they're blissed out: Paradise has enveloped their hearts, and they become determined to stay forever.

That is how many folks discover Hawai'i: They come on vacation and then realize this is where they really want to live. Yet Hawai'i's true nature is much more far-reaching and complex than one's first few deliciously seductive impressions. Relocating to the Islands is a big step—you must learn a whole new way of life.

People here operate on Hawaiian (or Island) time, which means that if you're late for a party, an appointment, a meeting, a dinner, or any other social function, you just don't worry about it. On Hawaiian time people take a much more laid-back approach to everything. This may be why residents here live longer than those in other states.

Living in Hawai'i teaches respect for nature. You stay out of the water when the huge winter waves come up on the north shores. You don't plan hiking trips in the valleys during rainy days when flash floods are possible. Windows get taped up before hurricanes as a precaution against strong, damaging winds. And when the sun starts to make its descent to the horizon, you stop what you're doing to enjoy the splendor of a Hawaiian sunset: It's a guaranteed spectacle almost every day of the year.

Natural Beauty

Hawai'i is America's most enticingly exotic and tropical state, with 132 islands and atolls stretching across some 1,600 mi of the South Seas. It is blessed with a uniform climate of predictably warm temperatures and cool trade winds; except for the occasional squalls of December, January, and February, the rains pass quickly. They say that clean de-ionized air comes all the way from the Arctic—with no pollutants to interrupt its path—and bathes these fragrant shores.

It's hard to believe that such a gentle place sprang from tremendously violent beginnings; the Islands emerged from the ocean as a result of continual volcanic eruptions. For centuries Hawai'i's fiery heights scorched the clouds; then for centuries more, wind and water erosion—crashing surf, mighty sea winds, and powerful rivers—carved and chiseled the great

mountains and lush valleys visible today.

The Past in the Present

With the Islands' cultural traditions paramount—and gaining importance—the old will never completely disappear. To this day the locals have a custom of blessing all things that are new by paying tribute to the past, with a dance, a chant, a lei, or even just a few words spoken by a minister. They respect the legends of their ancestors and honor the gods accordingly. Many Island customs can be learned and enjoyed by guests. One, of course, is the widely familiar, traditional lei greeting. Centuries ago, garlands of leaves, nuts, or flowers were offered to the gods; today they are a customary gift for family or friends on special occasions. Lei greetings can also be arranged for incoming visitors. It is said that the idea of bestowing a kiss along with a lei dates from World War II, when during a show a female entertainer smooched a soldier after draping him with a flower lei. Then she justified it by saying, "It's tradition in Hawai'i." It has been so ever since.

The past endures thanks to several concerned organizations that have been fighting to save the visible remnants of days gone by. For instance, a nonprofit group called the Historic Hawai'i Foundation works to preserve the state's unique, decades-old structures despite the new high-rises springing up around them.

The results are within plain view. In downtown Honolulu you can see the historic gem that is the 'Iolani Palace, dating from 1882. King Kalākaua commissioned this colonial-style building for his short but dynamic reign. The only official royal residence built on American soil, it has slowly but carefully been put back together inside and out, complete with many restored furnishings from its original days.

Cultural Potpourri

Not the least of Hawai'i's treasures are its people, who are open, fun-loving, and welcoming. From earliest times the Islands have beckoned to races from around the globe, beginning back when Polynesian kings and queens ruled these lands. Along the way, both Russia and France tried to claim Hawai'i as their own, as did Great Britain. Many modern residents are descended from people brought here to work on the Islands' sugar and pineapple plantations. They came from Japan, China, the Philippines, Korea, Vietnam, Samoa, Thailand, and Portugal, bringing with them their cultural traditions and turning Hawai'i into a Pacific melting pot.

Hawaiian customs still stand out in this cross-cultural mix. Highly cherished are the hula and chants, which have their roots in ancient Island history and have been handed down for centuries—in fact, the chants *are* the Islands' history, preserved in oral rather than written form. Today chants and hula are practiced almost religiously; in fact, children can learn hula in school. Each year enthusiastic audiences turn out to greet performers at hula festivals on the Big Island, O'ahu, and Maui.

Along with the swaying hips of the hula, the strumming sound of the 'ukulele has become innately associated with Hawai'i. The 'ukulele (the name means "jumping flea") was brought from Portugal by sugar-plantation workers. Today most every musical group that plays old-time Hawaiian songs includes a 'ukulele.

The Aloha Spirit

Hospitality is not a new feature of the Hawaiian lifestyle. Even in ancient times, community members who failed to welcome incoming guests were shunned by the rest of society. Since then it has been a revered Island custom that when people come to call, they are not treated like anonymous tourists but embraced as cherished guests or long-lost friends. In this very special way Hawai'i becomes everyone's home—each visitor is a new and welcome member of the family.

— Marty Wentzel

PLEASURES AND PASTIMES

Beaches

Waikīkī Beach *means* Hawai'i to most visitors. This hotel-studded strip of sand at the foot of Diamond Head sees its share of sun worshipers along what is actually a collection of smaller sections known as Ft. De Russy, Gray's, and Queen's Surf beaches. It's tough to beat for convenience to hotels, restaurants, and shopping. Also on O'ahu and synonymous with surfing the big waves are Kailua Beach Park, the site of international windsurfing competitions; neighboring Lanikai Beach, often referred to as the most beautiful beach in the world; and Makapu'u Beach, near Sea Life Park, which has some of the best bodysurfing in the state.

Dining

Hawai'i's melting-pot population accounts for its great variety of epicurean delights. In addition to American and Continental cuisines, you can choose from Hawaiian, Thai, Korean, Japanese, Chinese, Philippine, and Vietnamese. Many visitors rate their experience of a Hawaiian lū'au among the highlights of their stay.

Currently, chefs and fine restaurants are emphasizing Hawai'i Regional cuisine, with beautifully presented fresh-caught Island fish and the best of locally grown produce.

One of the trendiest places to dine in downtown Honolulu is at Aloha Tower Marketplace, in one of the numerous restaurants right on the water (a rarity on O'ahu). A trolley runs regularly between the marketplace and Waikīkī.

Lodging

O'ahu's diverse lodgings play to bigwigs, backpackers, and everyone in between. Waikīkī has the island's largest selection, from high-rise hotels to beachfront condos to four-story walk-ups away from the beach. Waikīkī is small enough that you don't have to pay a premium for a hotel *near* the beach. You can rent a little room three blocks from the ocean and still spend your days on the sand rubbing elbows with the rich and famous. First-time guests do well by this South Shore tourist mecca, since shopping, restaurants, nightlife, and the beach are all just a stroll away. Business travelers like to stay on the eastern edge of Waikīkī, near the new Hawai'i Convention Center, or in downtown Honolulu's sole hotel.

Lū'au

Just about everyone who comes to Hawai'i goes to at least one lū'au. Traditionally, the lū'au would last for days, with feasting, sporting events, hula, and song. But at today's scaled-down and, for the most part, inauthentic version, you're as likely to find macaroni salad on the buffet as poi (taroroot paste) and big heaps of fried chicken beside the platter of kālua pig. Traditional dishes that visitors actually enjoy include laulau, lomilomi salmon, and haupia. As for the notorious poi, the clean, bland taste goes nicely with something salty.

If you want authenticity, look in the newspaper to see if a church or civic club is holding a lū'au fund-raiser. You'll not only be welcome, you'll experience some down-home Hawaiiana.

Shopping

Honolulu is experiencing a retail boom. Many of the big mainland chains are here now, like Nieman Marcus, Nordstrom, and Niketown, and a complex of outlet stores west of Honolulu draws shoppers with big-name bargains. What makes shopping on O'ahu additionally interesting is the rich cultural diversity of its products and the many items unique to Hawai'i, such as bowls made of koa wood and jewelry fashioned from rare shells from the island of Ni'ihau. Waikīkī and Honolulu proper are particularly good places to find handmade Hawaiian souvenirs.

Water Sports

Whether you soar above them, sail on them, or dive into them, the waters surrounding O'ahu are teeming with activity. The seas off Waikīkī call to tourists looking for a surfing lesson and outrigger canoe ride. Snorkeling and scuba diving at Hanauma Bay, on the island's eastern tip, bring you face to face with a rainbow of sea creatures. Honolulu's Kewalo Basin is the starting point for most fishing charters. Windsurfers and ocean kayakers head to the beaches of the windward side, Lanikai in particular, for equipment rentals and lessons in near-perfect conditions. Year-round and island-wide, the water temperature is conducive to a dip, but don't so much as wade if the waves and currents are threatening.

NEW AND NOTEWORTHY

Good news for east coast travelers: At press time Continental Airlines was scheduled to begin nonstop flights from Newark to Honolulu in summer 1998.

The state-of-the-art Hawai'i Convention Center (HCC) in Waikīkī opened summer 1998. The HCC's 200,000-sq-ft exhibition space is expected to broaden the state's appeal as a business destination.

Honolulu's gone retail crazy! In Waikīkī, the 81,000-sq-ft Kalākaua Plaza opened in 1998 with such stores as Niketown and Banana Republic. Neiman Marcus and Nordstrom will add new luster to Ala Moana Shopping Center with their respective 1998 and 2000 openings.

The USS *Missouri* was towed from Bremerton, Washington to Pearl Harbor in mid-1998. The famed battleship will open as a museum and interactive educational center in January 1999, about 1,000 ft from the *Arizona* Memorial.

A new highway, which connects the windward side of the island with Pearl Harbor, opened December 12, 1997. The four-lane H-3 is reached from Honolulu via the Halawa Interchange, near Aloha Stadium.

2 Exploring Honolulu & Waikīkī

MORE AND MORE HAWAI'I RESIDENTS CLAIM that O'ahu is their favorite island, with the most spectacular scenery in all of Hawai'i. Part of its dramatic appearance lies in its majestic highlands: the western Wai'anae Mountains, which rise 4,000 ft above sea level, and the verdant Ko'olau Mountains, which cross the island's midsection at elevations of more than 3,000 ft. Eons of erosion by wind and weather have carved these ranges' sculptured, jagged peaks, deep valleys, sheer green cliffs, and dynamic vistas. At the base of these mountains more than 50 beach parks lie draped like a beautiful lei, each one known for a different ocean activity: snorkeling, bodysurfing, swimming, or windsurfing.

Updated by Marty Wentzel

Third largest of the Hawaiian Islands and covering 608 square mi, O'ahu was formed by two volcanoes that erupted 4–6 million years ago and, over time, created the peaceable kingdom we see today. Though 75% of Hawai'i's 1.1 million residents live on O'ahu, somehow there is also enough room for wide-open spaces and a pace that allows you sufficient time to take a deep breath and relax. Waikīkī is the center of the island's visitor industry, with its beachside strip of accommodations, stores, restaurants, nightclubs, and activities. Dominated by Diamond Head crater, Waikīkī's less populated eastern end includes a zoo and aquarium, and it encourages urban hiking and jogging. West of Waikīkī awaits Hawai'i's capital city of Honolulu, a bustling blend of history and modern-day commerce. The photogenic East O'ahu coast is fringed with white-sand beaches and turquoise seas, and it has a drive right over the top of the Ko'olau Mountains. Finally, a circle-island tour takes you to central, northern, and windward O'ahu, where shoes and cell phones give way to sandy toes and Hawaiian time.

Hawai'i's last kings and queens ruled from Honolulu's 'Iolani Palace, near the present downtown. It was at 'Iolani that the American flag first flew over the Islands. Even in those days of royalty, the virtues of Waikīkī as a vacation destination were recognized. Long processions of *ali'i* (nobility) made their way across streams and swamps, past the duck ponds, to the coconut groves and the beach.

By the 1880s, guest houses were scattered along the beach like seashells. The first hotel, the Moana (now the Sheraton Moana Surfrider), was built at the turn of the century. At that time Waikīkī was connected to the rest of Honolulu by tram, which brought townspeople to the shore. In 1927 the "Pink Palace of the Pacific," the Royal Hawaiian Hotel, was built by the Matson Navigation Company to accommodate travelers arriving on luxury liners. It was opened with a grand ball, and Waikīkī was launched as a first-class tourist destination: duck ponds, taro patches, and all. The rich and famous came from around the world. December 7, 1941, brought that era to a close, with the bombing of Pearl Harbor and America's entry into the war in the Pacific. The Royal Hawaiian was turned over to American forces and provided hundreds of war-weary soldiers and sailors with a warm welcome in Waikīkī.

With victory came the postwar boom. By 1952, Waikīkī had 2,000 hotel rooms. In 1969 there were 15,000. Today that figure has more than doubled. Hundreds of thousands of visitors now sleep in the more than 31,000 rooms of Waikīkī's nearly 120 hotels and condominiums. To this 1½-sq-mi Pacific playground come sun bunnies, honeymooners, marines on holiday, Europeans and Canadians with a lot of time to spend, Japanese, and every other type of tourist imaginable. With Waikīkī leading the way, O'ahu maintains its status as an exciting destination, with more things to see and do, and more places to eat than all the other Hawaiian Islands combined.

Directions on O'ahu are often given as *mauka*—toward the mountains, or *makai*—toward the ocean. You may also hear people referring to "Diamond Head"—toward that landmark; and *'ewa*—away from Diamond Head. You'll find these terms used throughout this section.

Waikīkī

If Hawai'i is America's most exotic, most unusual state, then Waikīkī is its generator, keeping everything humming. On the dry, sunny side of O'ahu, it incorporates all the natural splendors of the Islands and synthesizes them with elegance and daring into an international resort city in the middle of the vast blue Pacific.

A tropical playground since the days of Hawai'i's kings and queens, Waikīkī sparkles along 2½ mi of spangled sea from the famous Diamond Head crater on the east to the Ala Wai Yacht Harbor on the west. Separated on its northern boundary from the sprawling city of Honolulu by the broad Ala Wai Canal, Waikīkī is 3½ mi from downtown Honolulu and worlds apart from any other city in the world. Nowhere else is there such a salad of cultures so artfully tossed, each one retaining its distinct flavor and texture. Even McDonald's is multi-ethnic, with burgers next to *saimin* (noodle soup). You'll find yourself saying things like aloha and *mahalo* (thank you), and you'll encounter almost as many sushi bars as ice-cream stands.

Numbers in the text correspond to numbers in the margin and on the Honolulu Including Waikīkī, Waikīkī, Downtown Honolulu, and O'ahu maps.

A Good Walk

A good place to start a Waikīkī walking tour is from the **Ala Wai Yacht Harbor** ①, home to an armada of pleasure boats and two members-only yacht clubs. It's just makai of the 'Ilikai Hotel Nikko Waikīkī at 1777 Ala Moana Boulevard. From here head toward the main intersection of Ala Moana Boulevard and Kālia Road, turn right at the big sign to **Hilton Hawaiian Village** ②, and wander through this lush, 20-acre resort complex past gardens and waterfalls.

Continue makai on Kālia Road to Ft. DeRussy, home of the **U.S. Army Museum** ③ and its display of wartime artifacts. Across the street, on Saratoga Road, nestled snugly amid the commerce of Waikīkī, is an oasis of tranquillity: the **Tea House of the Urasenke Foundation** ④, an offshoot of a centuries-old institution based in Kyoto, Japan. Take part in an authentic Japanese tea ceremony; you'll be served tea and sweets by kimono-clad ladies.

With a little zip from the tea and some Zen for the road, head mauka until you reach Kalākaua Avenue, then turn toward Diamond Head. At the intersection with Lewers Street, stop and peer into the lobby of the **First Hawaiian**

Bank ⑤; you'll spy six massive murals portraying the indigenous peoples of Hawai'i and their cultural history. Diagonally across Kalākaua Avenue is one of Waikīkī's architectural landmarks, the **Gump Building** ⑥.

Walk down Lewers Street toward the ocean. It dead-ends at the impressive **Halekūlani** ⑦, one of Waikīkī's most prestigious hotels, famed for its elegant hospitality. From the Halekūlani stroll toward Diamond Head along the paved oceanside walkway. It leads past the Sheraton Waikīkī to the gracious, historic, and very pink **Royal Hawaiian Hotel** ⑧. It is hidden from Kalākaua Avenue by the three-story Royal Hawaiian Shopping Center. Back on the mauka side of Kalākaua Avenue, walk two blocks 'ewa and one block mauka to the **Hawai'i IMAX Theater** ⑨, home of continuous huge-screen films, including a great one about Hawai'i. Return to Kalākaua and walk toward Diamond Head. Your next stop on the mauka side of the street is the **International Market Place** ⑩, a tropical tangle of 200 shops under a spreading banyan complete with its own Swiss Family Robinson–style tree house—shopping is part of the adventure in Waikīkī. Continue heading toward Diamond Head to reach the Hyatt Regency Waikīkī. This sleek high-rise hotel is notable for its small second-floor museum of artifacts, quilts, and crafts called **Hyatt's Hawai'i** ⑪.

Across Kalākaua Avenue is the oldest hotel in Waikīkī, the venerable **Sheraton Moana Surfrider** ⑫. Wander through the breezy lobby to the wide back porch, called the Banyan Veranda, that overlooks the beach. From here, walk down to the beach and head toward Diamond Head. At the beach showers next to Kalakaua Avenue you'll find the four **Kahuna (Wizard) Stones of Waikīkī** ⑬. Said to hold magical powers, they are often overlooked and, more often than not, irreverently draped in wet towels.

If you walk along Kalakaua Avenue four blocks farther toward Diamond Head then turn mauka onto 'Ōhua Avenue you'll find the only church in Waikīkī with its own building, the Roman Catholic St. Augustine's. In the back of the church is the **Damien Museum** ⑭, a small but fascinating two-room exhibit centering on the life and work of the Belgian priest Father Joseph Damien de Veuster. Father Damien came to Hawai'i and labored and died while ministering to victims of Hansen's disease (leprosy) on the island of Molokaʻi.

TIMING

A world unto itself, Waikīkī can take days to explore. If you're looking for T-shirts or souvenirs, you can spend several hours at the Royal Hawaiian Shopping Center alone. Perusing the Damien Museum will take a half hour and the U.S. Army Museum an hour, if you're so inclined. To fully appreciate the Tea House of the Urasenke Foundation, allow yourself an hour.

Many shops and attractions are open every day of the year from sunup to way past sundown, to cater to the body clocks and pocketbooks of tourists from around the world. Still, Waikīkī is most inviting in the cool of the early morning. Until 9:30 or 10 AM there's less traffic to contend with, fewer people on the sidewalks, and more room on the beach. The weather is sunny and pleasant almost every day of the year, so you'll rarely need a jacket or umbrella.

Allow yourself at least one full day for this walk, and time it so that you'll wind up on Waikīkī Beach at sunset.

Sights to See

① Ala Wai Yacht Harbor. Every other summer the Trans-Pacific yacht race from Los Angeles makes its colorful finish here, complete with flags and on-board parties; it will next arrive July 1999. Stroll around the docks and check out the variety of craft, from houseboats to luxury cruisers. ⊠ *1777 Ala Moana Blvd., ocean side across from ʻIlikai Hotel Nikko Waikīkī.*

⑭ Damien Museum. Browse the low-key exhibits about Father Damien, the priest who worked with the lepers of Molokaʻi during the late 1800s, and ask to see the museum's 20-minute videotape. It is low budget, but well done and emotionally gripping. ⊠ *130 ʻŌhua Ave.,* ☎ *808/923–2690.* ▤ *Free.* ☺ *Weekdays 9–3.*

⑤ First Hawaiian Bank. Art, not commerce, may seem to take precedence at this bank: Half a dozen murals depict the evolution of Hawaiian culture, from Hawaiian arts before contact with the Western world to the introduction of the first printing press to the Islands in 1872. The impressive

Honolulu Including Waikīkī

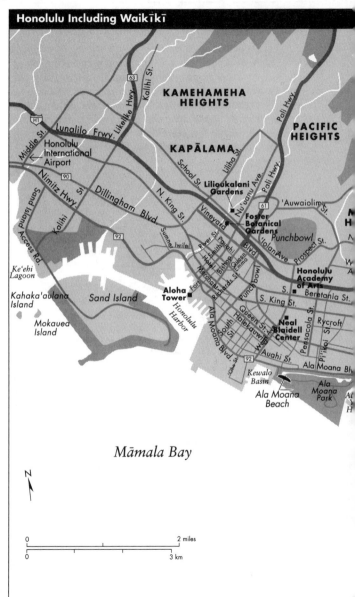

KAMEHAMEHA HEIGHTS

PACIFIC HEIGHTS

Lunalilo Frwy.

Likelike Hwy.

Kalihi St.

63

H1

Middle St.

Honolulu International Airport

90

Nimitz Hwy.

Dillingham Blvd.

N. King St.

School St.

KAPĀLAMA

Liliha St.

Poli Hwy.

'Auwaiolimu St.

Sand Island Access Rd.

Kolihi

Ke'ehi Lagoon

Kahaka'aulana Island

Mokauea Island

Sand Island

92

Iwilei

Summer

River St.

Pauahi

N. Smith St.

Hotel

Bishop

Merchant

Richards St.

Fort

Queen

Ala Moana Blvd.

Halekauwila

South St.

Queen St.

Avahi St.

92

Ala Moana Blvd.

Vineyard

Lilioukalani Gardens

Foster Botanical Gardens

61

Nu'uanu Ave.

'Iolani Ave.

Beretania Blvd.

Prospect St.

Punchbowl St.

S. Emma

Punchbowl

Honolulu Academy of Arts

Beretania St.

S. King St.

Neal Blaidell Center

Pensacola St.

Rycroft

Pi'ikoi St.

Ala Moana Blvd.

Ala Moana Park

Aloha Tower

Honolulu Harbor

Kewalo Basin

Ala Moana Beach

Māmala Bay

N

0 — 2 miles

0 — 3 km

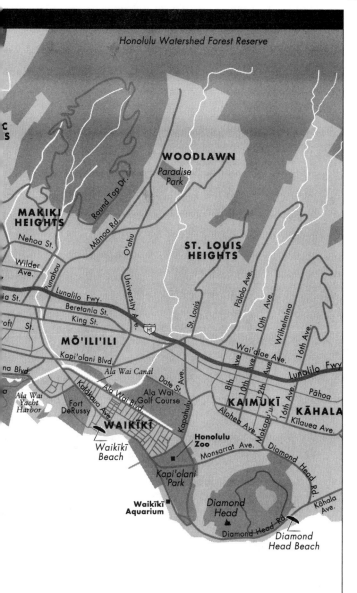

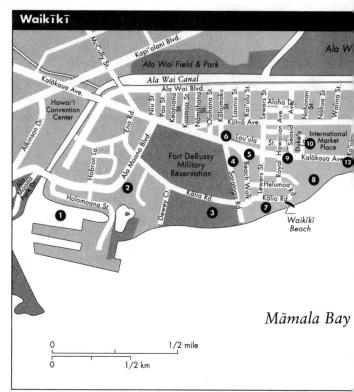

Waikīkī

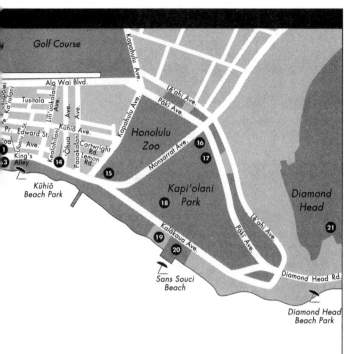

Royal Hawaiian
Hotel, **8**

Sheraton Moana
Surfrider, **12**

Tea House
of the Urasenke
Foundation, **4**

U.S. Army
Museum, **3**

Waikīkī
Aquarium, **19**

Waikīkī Shell, **16**

Waikīkī War
Memorial
Natatorium, **20**

panels were painted between 1951 and '52 by Jean Char-
lot (1898–1979), whose work is represented in Florence
at the Uffizi Gallery and in New York at both the Metropoli-
tan Museum and the Museum of Modern Art. The murals
are beautifully lit at night, with some panels visible from
the street. ⊠ *2181 Kalākaua Ave.,* ☎ *808/943–4670.* 🌐
Free. ☉ *Mon.–Thurs. 8:30–3, Fri. 8:30–6.*

❻ **Gump Building.** Built in 1929 in Hawaiian-colonial style,
with Asian architectural motifs and a blue-tile roof, the structure that once housed Hawai'i's premier store, Gump's
(known for high-quality Asian and Hawaiian objects), has
been replaced by a branch of Louis Vuitton. ⊠ *2200
Kalākaua Ave.*

❼ **Halekūlani.** Incorporated into this relatively new hotel is
a portion of its old (1917) structure, which was the setting
for the first of the Charlie Chan detective novels, *The
House Without a Key.* Today one of the most appealing
things about the hotel, aside from its famed restaurants, is
the gigantic floral arrangement in the lobby. Take a peek
at the swimming pool with its huge orchid mosaic on the
bottom. ⊠ *2199 Kālia Rd.,* ☎ *808/923–2311.*

☙ ❾ **Hawai'i IMAX Theater.** Immerse yourself in what's on a
screen five stories high and 70 ft wide while surrounding
you with digital stereo sound. Show subjects and times vary.
⊠ *325 Seaside Ave.,* ☎ *808/923–4629.* 🌐 *$7.50, 2 films
on same day $10, 3 films $12.* ☉ *Daily 9–9.*

❷ **Hilton Hawaiian Village.** For sure, this is the picture of a
quintessential tropical getaway, complete with a little island
in Kahanamoku Lagoon and palm trees all around. Look
for the penguin pond in the back of the main lobby. The
village is a hodgepodge of Asian architecture, with a Chinese moon gate, a pagoda, and a Japanese farmhouse with
a waterwheel, all dominated by a tall mosaic mural of the
hotel's Rainbow Tower. The **Rainbow Bazaar** here is a
good place to browse for souvenirs. ⊠ *2005 Kālia Rd.,* ☎
808/949–4321.

⓫ **Hyatt's Hawai'i.** To help visitors become acquainted with
Hawaiian arts and crafts, Aunty Malia, resident Hawaiian
authority for the Hyatt Regency Waikīkī, has assembled what
she calls her "sharing place." It's a charming collection, and

she's a one-of-a-kind Hawai'i resource. ⊠ *Hyatt Regency Waikīkī, 2424 Kalākaua Ave., 2nd floor,* ☎ *808/923–1234.* ☉ *Daily 9 AM–11 PM.*

🔟 **International Market Place.** The tropical open-air setting is fun to wander through, with wood-carvers, basket-weavers, and other artisans from various Pacific islands hawking their handicrafts. ⊠ *2330 Kalākaua Ave.,* ☎ *808/923–9871.*

⓭ **Kahuna (Wizard) Stones of Waikīkī.** According to legend, these boulders preserve the magnetic legacy of four sorcerers—Kapaemahu, Kinohi, Kapuni, and Kahaloa—who came here from Tahiti sometime before the 16th century. Before leaving the Islands they transferred their mystic knowledge and healing powers to these rock-solid totems. Just to the west of these revered rocks is the **Duke Kahanamoku Statue,** erected in honor of Hawai'i's celebrated surfer and swimmer. Known as the "father of modern surfing," Duke won a gold medal for the 100-meter freestyle at the 1912 Olympics. ⊠ *Waikīkī Beach, Diamond Head side of Sheraton Moana Surfrider.*

⑧ **Royal Hawaiian Hotel.** Affectionately nicknamed the Pink Palace, the Royal Hawaiian was built in 1927. The lobby, with its pink decor, is reminiscent of another era when visitors to the Islands arrived on luxury liners. A stroll through the old gardens with their tall, swaying coconut palms is like a walk through a time when Waikīkī was a sleepy, tropical paradise with only two luxury hotels. ⊠ *2259 Kalākaua Ave.,* ☎ *808/923–7311.*

⓬ **Sheraton Moana Surfrider.** This renovated landmark dates from 1901; it has period furnishings, historical exhibits, and plenty of nostalgia. They've done a beautiful job on this Beaux Arts–style hotel, which has been placed on the National Register of Historic Places. Visit the **Historical Room** in the rotunda above the main entrance to enjoy a collection of old photographs and memorabilia dating from the opening of the hotel. Then have a drink on the back **Banyan Veranda.** ⊠ *2365 Kalākaua Ave.,* ☎ *808/922–3111.*

④ **Tea House of the Urasenke Foundation.** This teahouse was the first of its kind to be built outside Japan and provides an excellent introduction to Japanese culture. Wear something comfortable enough for sitting on the floor (but no shorts, please). ⊠ *245 Saratoga Rd.,* ☎ *808/923–3059.* ☎ *Minimum donation $2.* ☉ *Wed. and Fri. 10 AM–noon.*

☾ ❸ **U.S. Army Museum.** This museum at Ft. DeRussy houses an intimidating collection of war paraphernalia. The major focus is on World War II memorabilia, but exhibits range from ancient Hawaiian weaponry to displays relating to the Vietnam War. It's within Battery Randolph (Building 32), a bunker built in 1911 as a key to the defense of Pearl Harbor and Honolulu. Some of its walls are 22 ft thick. Guided group tours can be arranged. ⊠ *Ft. DeRussy, Bldg. 32, Kālia Rd.,* ☎ *808/438–2821.* ☎ *Free.* ☉ *Tues.–Sun. 10–4:30.*

Kapi'olani Park and Diamond Head

Established during the late 1800s by King Kalākaua and named after his queen, Kapi'olani Park is a 500-acre expanse where you can play all sorts of sports, enjoy a picnic, see wild animals, or hear live music. It lies in the shadow of Diamond Head, Hawai'i's most famous natural landmark. Diamond Head got its name from sailors who thought they had found precious gems on its slopes; the diamonds proved to be volcanic refuse.

A Good Walk

The 'ewa end of Kapi'olani Park is occupied by the **Honolulu Zoo** ⑮, on the corner of Kalākaua and Kapahulu avenues. Its 40 acres are home to 2,000 furry and finned creatures. On weekends look for the Zoo Fence Art Mart, on Monsarrat Avenue outside the zoo, on the Diamond Head side. You might find some affordable works by contemporary artists and craftspeople that make better Hawai'i keepsakes than the ashtrays and monkeypod bowls carved in the Philippines.

Across Monsarrat Avenue, between Kalākaua Avenue and Pākī Street in Kapi'olani Park, is the **Waikīkī Shell** ⑯, Honolulu's outdoor concert arena. Next to the Shell is the site of the **Kodak Hula Show** ⑰, a free presentation of Hawaiian song and dance. Cut across the park to the **Kapi'olani Bandstand** ⑱, where you'll hear more free island tunes.

Cross Kalākaua Avenue to the **Waikīkī Aquarium** ⑲. Next door is the **Waikīkī War Memorial Natatorium** ⑳, an open-

air swimming stadium-by-the-sea built in 1927 to com-
memorate lives lost in World War I.

As it leaves Kapi'olani Park, Kalākaua Avenue forks into
Diamond Head Road, a scenic 2-mi stretch popular with
walkers and joggers. The road climbs a steep hill and passes
handsome Diamond Head Lighthouse (not open to the
public). Lookout areas along the top of the hill offer views
of the surfers and windsurfers below.

For those willing to undertake more strenuous walking, the
hike to the summit of **Diamond Head** ㉑ offers a marvelous
view. To save time and energy, drive, don't walk, along Diamond Head Road, turn left at Monsarrat Avenue, head a
mile up the hill, and look for a sign on the left to the entrance to the crater. Drive through the tunnel to the inside
of the crater. The trail begins at the parking lot.

TIMING
Budget a full day to see Kapi'olani Park and Diamond
Head. The park is particularly nice in the early morning
when only a few joggers and walkers are around; walking
around the rim of the park is easiest before 9 AM. If you
want to hike up to the crater's summit, do it before breakfast. That way you beat not only the heat but the crowds.
Hiking Diamond Head takes an hour round-trip, but fac-
tor in some extra time to enjoy the views from the top. Keep
an eye on your watch if you're there at day's end, because
the gates close promptly at 6 PM. If you want to see the Honolulu Zoo, it's best to go there right when it opens, since
the animals are livelier in the cool of the morning. Give the
aquarium an hour, including 10 minutes in its Sea Vision
Theater. For the best seats at the 10 AM Kodak Hula Show,
get there by 9. Unless you're visiting around the Thanks-
giving or Christmas holidays, you'll have no trouble getting into all of the following sights, with the exception of
the Kodak Hula Show, which runs Tuesday through Thursday only.

Sights to See

㉑ **Diamond Head.** Once a military fortification, this 760-ft
extinct volcanic peak provides the ideal perspective for
first-time O'ahu visitors. From its height, panoramas sweep
across Waikīkī and Honolulu in one direction and out to

Koko Head in the other, with surfers and windsurfers scattered like confetti on the cresting waves below. Most guidebooks say there are 99 steps on the trail to the top. That's true of one flight, but there are four flights altogether. Bring a flashlight to see your way through a narrow tunnel and up a very dark flight of winding stairs. ⊠ *Monsarrat Ave.* ⊠ *Free.* ⊗ *Daily 6–6.*

🖐 ⑮ **Honolulu Zoo.** There are bigger and better zoos, but this one is pretty, and on Wednesday evenings in summer, the zoo puts on "The Wildest Show in Town," a free program of singing, dancing, and island entertainment; check the local newspaper. The best part of the zoo is its 7½-acre African savanna, where animals roam freely on the other side of hidden rails and moats. ⊠ *151 Kapahulu Ave.,* ☎ *808/971–7171.* ⊠ *$6.* ⊗ *Daily 9–4:30.*

⑱ **Kapi'olani Bandstand.** There's usually a free show of some kind at this open-air stage; on Sunday at 2, for instance, it's the Royal Hawaiian Band. Check the newspaper for particulars. Some excellent hula dances are performed here by local groups that don't frequent the hotels. ⊠ *'Ewa end of Kapi'olani Park, mauka side of Kalākaua Ave.*

⑰ **Kodak Hula Show.** This one-hour show, in the bleachers adjacent to the Waikīkī Shell, is colorful, lively, and fun; it's been wowing crowds for more than 50 years. Naturally, it's a great opportunity to take photographs. ⊠ *2805 Monsarrat Ave.,* ☎ *808/627–3379.* ⊠ *Free.* ⊗ *Tues.–Thurs. at 10 AM.*

🖐 ⑲ **Waikīkī Aquarium.** This amazing little attraction harbors more than 300 species of Hawaiian and South Pacific marine life, including the giant clam, the chambered nautilus, and sharks. Check out the Sea Visions Theater, whose 10-minute films enhance the current exhibits. ⊠ *2777 Kalākaua Ave.,* ☎ *808/923–9741.* ⊠ *$6.* ⊗ *Daily 9–5.*

⑯ **Waikīkī Shell.** Local people bring a picnic and get "grass seats" (lawn seating). Here's a chance to have a magical night listening to some of Hawai'i's best musicians and visiting pop stars, while lying on a blanket with the moon shining over Diamond Head. Most concerts are held between May 1 and Labor Day. Check the newspapers to see what's playing. ⊠ *2805 Monsarrat Ave.,* ☎ *808/924–8934.*

20 Waikīkī War Memorial Natatorium. Although it has fallen into disrepair and is no longer open to the public, this World War I monument stands proudly, its outer wall lighted at night, showing off what's left of the pair of eagle statues that sits atop the entrance. Built in 1927, the natatorium narrowly escaped the wrecker's ball but continues to await restoration. ⊠ 2777 *Kalākaua Ave., Diamond Head side of Waikīkī Aquarium.*

Downtown Honolulu

Honolulu's past and present play a delightful counterpoint throughout the downtown sector. Modern skyscrapers stand directly across from the Aloha Tower, which was built in 1926. Old structures have found new meaning here. For instance, today's governor's mansion, built in 1846, was the home of Queen Lili'uokalani until her death in 1917.

To reach downtown Honolulu from Waikīkī by car, take Ala Moana Boulevard to Alakea Street. There are public parking lots (50¢ per half hour) in buildings along Alakea Street and Bethel Street, two blocks 'ewa. Keep in mind that parking in most downtown lots is expensive ($2 per half hour).

If you travel by public transportation, take Bus 19 or 20 from Kuhio Avenue in Waikīkī. After about 15 minutes, get off at Alakea Street and walk makai to Ala Moana Boulevard. Most of the historic sites are clustered within easy walking distance.

A Good Walk

Begin at the **Hawai'i Maritime Center** 22, which is across Ala Moana Boulevard from Alakea Street in downtown Honolulu. The lively oceanfront museum traces the history of Hawai'i's love affair with the sea.

Just 'ewa of the Hawai'i Maritime Center is **Aloha Tower Marketplace** 23, a complex of harborside shops and restaurants where you can shop 'til you drop, have a drink and a bite to eat, and listen to live music.

Cross Ala Moana Boulevard, walk a block 'ewa, and turn mauka on Ft. Street Mall, a pedestrian walkway that passes buildings old and new. Sit on a bench for a few minutes

Downtown Honolulu

and watch the fascinating passing parade, from business-people to street preachers. Turn left on King Street, and in a few blocks you'll reach **Chinatown** ㉔, the old section of downtown Honolulu, which is crammed with mom-and-pop shops, art galleries, ethnic restaurants, and a big open market.

Walk back toward Diamond Head along King Street until it intersects with Bishop Street. On the mauka side is lovely **Tamarind Park** ㉕, a popular lunchtime picnic spot for Honolulu's workforce, which gathers under its shady plumeria, *kukui,* and monkeypod trees—and one tamarind.

Continue along King Street until you reach **ʻIolani Palace** ㉖, on the mauka side. This graceful Victorian structure was built by King David Kalākaua in 1882. Take a guided tour of the restored interior, then stop at the ʻIolani Barracks. Also on the palace grounds is the Kalākaua Coronation Bandstand, where the Royal Hawaiian Band performs at noon most Fridays.

Across King Street from ʻIolani Palace is Aliʻiōlani Hale, the old judiciary building that served as the parliament hall during the kingship era. In front of it is the gilded **Kamehameha I Statue** ㉗, which honors Hawaiʻi's greatest monarch.

Walk one block mauka up Richards Street to tour the **Hawaiʻi State Capitol** ㉘, where Hawaiʻi's legislators spend their days. Almost across the street from the state capitol is Washington Place, a graceful old mansion and currently the home of Hawaiʻi's governor. You can only peer through the wrought-iron gates, since the residence is not open to the public.

Return to King Street, stay on the mauka side, and proceed in a Diamond Head direction. Past the palace is the massive stone **Hawaiʻi State Library** ㉙, built in 1913 and renovated in 1992, a showcase of architectural restoration.

On the mauka side of South King Street, at Punchbowl Street, is **Honolulu Hale** ㉚, or City Hall. Across the street, on another corner of King and Punchbowl streets, is the **Kawaiahaʻo Church** ㉛, Hawaiʻi's most famous religious structure. On the Diamond Head side of the Kawaiahaʻo Church is the **Mission Houses Museum** ㉜, where the first American missionaries in Hawai'i lived.

From here it's three long blocks toward Diamond Head to Ward Avenue and one block mauka to Beretania Street, but the **Honolulu Academy of Arts** ㉝ is worth the extra mileage (you might choose to drive there instead); it houses a world-class collection of Western and Asian art.

TIMING

Downtown Honolulu merits a full day of your time, especially if you set aside a half day for Aloha Tower Marketplace. Be sure to stop by the palace Tuesday through Saturday, the only days tours are offered. Remember that the Mission Houses Museum and Honolulu Academy of Arts are closed Monday. Touring the State Capitol can take up to two hours and is only possible during the week. Saturday morning is the best time to walk through Chinatown; that's when the open-air markets do their biggest business with local families. A walk through Chinatown can take an hour, as do tours of the Mission Houses and 'Iolani Palace.

Wrap up your day at sunset with refreshments or dinner back at the Aloha Tower Marketplace, which stays open late into the evening, with live entertainment on the docks.

Sights to See

🖐 ㉓ **Aloha Tower Marketplace.** This is a two-story conglomeration of shops, kiosks, indoor and outdoor restaurants, and live entertainment next to Honolulu Harbor, with Aloha Tower as its anchor. For a bird's-eye view of this working harbor, take the free ride up to the tower's observation deck. ⊠ *101 Ala Moana Blvd., at Piers 8, 9, and 10,* ☎ *808/528–5700 or 800/378–6937.*

㉔ **Chinatown.** Slightly on the tawdry side, this historic neighborhood has everything from art galleries in renovated structures to lei stands, herb shops, acupuncture studios, noodle factories, and Chinese and Thai restaurants. A major highlight is the colorful O'ahu Market, an open-air emporium with hanging pig heads, display cases of fresh fish, row after row of exotic fruits and vegetables, and vendors of all ethnic backgrounds. ⊠ *King St., between Smith and River Sts.*

🖑 ㉒ **Hawai'i Maritime Center.** The main exhibits (some of which are interactive) are in the **Kalākaua Boat House,** where you learn about such topics as Hawai'i's whaling days, the history of Honolulu Harbor, the Clipper seaplane, and surfing and windsurfing in Hawai'i. Also at the Center are the *Falls of Clyde,* a century-old, four-masted, square-rigged ship now used as a museum, and the *Hōkūle'a,* a reproduction of an ancient double-hull voyaging canoe. *Hōkūle'a* has completed several journeys throughout the Pacific, during which the crew used only the stars and the sea as their guide. ⊠ *Pier 7, Ala Moana Blvd.,* ☎ *808/536–6373.* ▨ *$7.50.* ☉ *Daily 8:30–5.*

㉘ **Hawai'i State Capitol.** The capitol's architecture is richly symbolic: The columns look like palm trees, the legislative chambers are shaped like volcanic cinder cones, and the central court is open to the sky, representing Hawai'i's open society. The building is surrounded by reflecting pools, just as the Islands are embraced by water. ⊠ *215 S. Beretania St.,* ☎ *808/586–0178.* ▨ *Free.* ☉ *1- to 2-hr guided tour weekdays at 1:30.*

㉙ **Hawai'i State Library.** This beautifully renovated main library is wonderful to explore. Its "Asia and the Pacific" room has a fascinating collection of books old and new about Hawai'i. ⊠ *478 King St.,* ☎ *808/586–3500.* ▨ *Free.* ☉ *Mon., Fri., and Sat. 9–5; Tues. and Thurs. 9–8; Wed. 10–5.*

㉝ **Honolulu Academy of Arts.** Dating to 1927, the Academy has an impressive permanent collection including Japanese prints, Italian Renaissance paintings, and American and European art. Six open-air courtyards provide a casual counterpart to the more formal interior galleries. Call about special exhibits, concerts, and films. ⊠ *900 S. Beretania St.,* ☎ *808/ 532–8700.* ▨ *$5.* ☉ *Tues.–Sat. 10–4:30; Sun. 1–5.*

㉚ **Honolulu Hale.** Center of city government, this Mediterranean/Renaissance-style building was constructed in 1929. Stroll through the cool, open-ceiling lobby with exhibits of local artists, and time your visit to coincide with one of the free live concerts sometimes offered in the evening, when the building stays open later. ⊠ *530 S. King St.,* ☎ *808/ 527–5666.* ▨ *Free.* ☉ *Weekdays 8–4:30.*

26 **ʻIolani Palace.** Built in 1882 on the site of an earlier palace and beautifully restored today, this is America's only royal residence. It contains the thrones of King Kalākaua and his successor (and sister) Queen Liliʻuokalani. The palace is open for guided tours only; reservations are essential. Take a look at the gift shop, formerly the ʻIolani Barracks, built to house the Royal Guard. ⊠ *King and Richards Sts.,* ☎ *808/ 522–0832.* ⊡ *$8.* ☉ *Tues.–Sat. 9–2:15.*

27 **Kamehameha I Statue.** This downtown landmark pays tribute to the Big Island chieftain who united all the warring Hawaiian Islands into one kingdom. He stands with one arm outstretched in welcome. The original version is in Kapaʻau, on the Big Island, near the king's birthplace. Each year on June 11, his birthday, the statue is draped in leis. ⊠ *417 S. King St., outside Aliʻiōlani Hale.*

31 **Kawaiahaʻo Church.** Fancifully called Hawaiʻi's Westminster Abbey, this coral-block house of worship witnessed the coronations, weddings, and funerals of generations of Hawaiian royalty. The graves of missionaries and of King Lunalilo are in the yard. The upper gallery has an exhibit of paintings of the royal families. Services in English and Hawaiian are given each Sunday. While there are no guided tours, you can look around the church at no cost. ⊠ *957 Punchbowl St., at King St.,* ☎ *808/522–1333.* ☉ *Service Sun. at 8 and 10:30, Wed. at 6* PM.

32 **Mission Houses Museum.** The stalwart Hawaiʻi missionaries arrived in 1820, gaining royal favor and influencing every aspect of Island life. Their descendants have become leaders in government and business. You can walk through their original dwellings, including a white-frame house that was prefabricated in New England and shipped around the Horn. ⊠ *553 S. King St.,* ☎ *808/531–0481.* ⊡ *$5.* ☉ *Tues.–Sat. 9–4, Sun. 12:30–4; certain areas of museum may be seen only on 1-hr guided tour, Tues.–Sat. at 9:30, 10:30, 11:30, 1, 2, and 3 and Sun. at 1, 2, and 3.*

25 **Tamarind Park.** From jazz and Hawaiian tunes to the U.S. Marine Band, music fills this pretty park at noon on Friday. Check the newspaper to find out the schedule. Do as the locals do: Pick up lunch at one of the many carry-out restaurants bordering the park and find a bench or patch of grass and enjoy. ⊠ *S. King St., between Bishop and Alakea Sts.* ☎ *Free.*

The East O'ahu Ring

At once historic and contemporary, serene and active, the east end of O'ahu holds remarkable variety within its relatively small area, and its scenery includes windswept cliffs and wave-dashed shores. For this drive, don't forget the camera!

A Good Drive

From Waikīkī there are two routes to Lunalilo Freeway (H-1). On the Diamond Head end, go mauka on Kapahulu Avenue and follow the signs to the freeway. On the 'ewa end, take Ala Wai Boulevard and turn mauka at Kalākaua Avenue, staying on it until it ends at Beretania Street, which is one-way going left. Turn right off Beretania Street at Pi'ikoi Street, and the signs will direct you onto the freeway heading west.

Take the freeway exit marked Pali Highway (Hwy. 61), one of two roads that cut through the Ko'olau Mountains. On the right is the **Queen Emma Summer Palace** ㉞. The colonial-style white mansion, which once served as the summer retreat of King Kamehameha IV and his wife, Queen Emma, is now a museum maintained by the Daughters of Hawai'i.

As you drive toward the summit of the highway, the road is lined with sweet ginger in summer and red poinsettias in winter. If it has been raining, waterfalls will be tumbling down the sheer, chiseled cliffs of the Ko'olau, creating a veritable wonderland in green.

Watch for the turn to the **Nu'uanu Pali Lookout** ㉟. There is a small parking lot and a lookout wall from which you can see all the way up and down the windward coast—a view that Mark Twain called the most beautiful in the world.

As you follow the highway down the other side of the mountain, continue straight along what becomes Kailua Road. If you are interested in Hawaiian history, look for the YMCA at the Castle Hospital junction of Kalaniana'ole Highway and Kailua Road. Behind it is **Ulupō Heiau** ㊱, an ancient outdoor shrine. Ready for a detour? Head straight

O'ahu

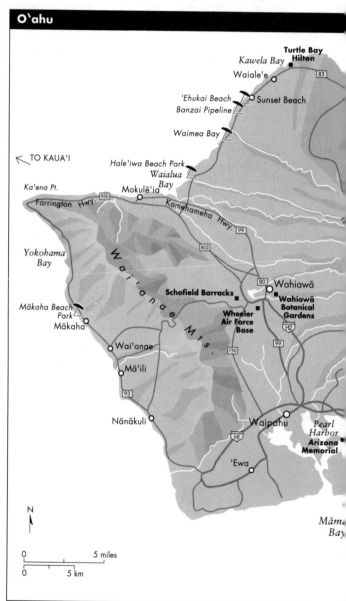

Turtle Bay Hilton

Kawela Bay

Waiale'e

83

'Ehukai Beach
Banzai Pipeline

Sunset Beach

Waimea Bay

← TO KAUA'I

Hale'iwa Beach Park
Waialua Bay

Ka'ena Pt.

Mokulē'ia

930

Farrington Hwy.

Kamehameha Hwy.

99

*Yokohama
Bay*

803

W
a
i
a
n
a
e

80 Wahiawā

Schofield Barracks

**Wahiawā
Botanical
Gardens**

*Mākaha Beach
Park*

Mākaha

**Wheeler
Air Force
Base**

H2

Wai'anae

M
t
s

750

99

Mā'ili

93

Nānākuli

Waipahu

*Pearl
Harbor*

**Arizona
Memorial**

H1

'Ewa

N

*Mām
Bay*

0   5 miles

0   5 km

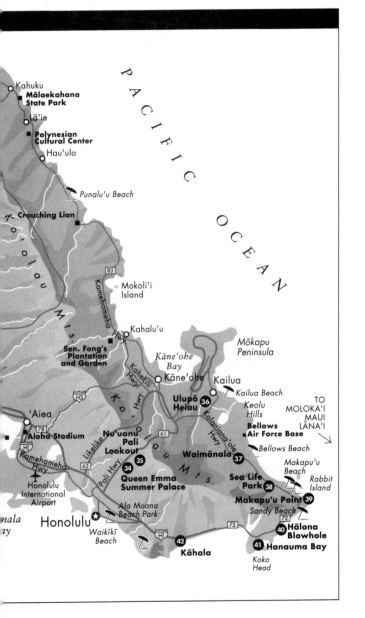

PACIFIC OCEAN

Kahuku
Mālaekahana State Park
Lā'ie
Polynesian Cultural Center
Hau'ula
Punalu'u Beach
Crouching Lion

Koʻolau Mts.

Kamehameha Hwy.
83
Mokoli'i Island
Kahalu'u
Sen. Fong's Plantation and Garden
Kāne'ohe Bay
Kāne'ohe
Kailua
Kailua Beach
Mōkapu Peninsula
H3
Kahekili Hwy.
Keolu Hills
'Aiea
78
Aloha Stadium
Ulupō Heiau 36
Kalaniana'ole Hwy.
TO MOLOKA'I MAUI LĀNA'I
Bellows Air Force Base
Bellows Beach
H1
Nu'uanu Pali Lookout
61
Likelike Hwy.
Kamehameha Hwy.
Honolulu International Airport
63
Queen Emma Summer Palace
34 35
Pali Hwy.
Waimānalo 37
Makapu'u Beach
Rabbit Island
Sea Life Park 38
Makapu'u Point 39
nala ay
Honolulu
Waikīkī Beach
Ala Moana Beach Park
H1
42
Kāhala
72
Sandy Beach
72
40 **Hālona Blowhole**
41 **Hanauma Bay**
Koko Head

on Kailua Road to Kailua Beach Park (☞ Beaches *in* Chapter 6), which many people consider the best on the island. The road twists and turns, so watch the signs.

Retracing your route back to Castle Junction, turn left at the intersection onto Kalaniana'ole Highway. Soon you will come to the simple town of **Waimānalo** ㊲. Waimānalo's two beaches are Bellows Beach, great for swimming and bodysurfing, and Waimānalo Beach Park (☞ Beaches *in* Chapter 6), also safe for swimming.

Another mile along the highway, on the right, is **Sea Life Park** ㊳, home to the world's only "wholphin," the offspring of a romance between a whale and a dolphin. From the cliffs above Sea Life Park, colorful hang gliders often soar in the breezes. It takes a lot of daring to leap from these imposing heights, and there have been several fatalities here.

Across the highway from Sea Life Park is Makapu'u Beach (☞ Beaches *in* Chapter 6), a beautiful cove that is great for seasoned bodysurfers but treacherous for the weak swimmer. The road winds up a hill, at the top of which is a turnoff on the makai side to **Makapu'u Point** ㊴, a fabulous photo opportunity.

Next you'll see a long stretch of inviting sand called Sandy Beach (☞ Beaches *in* Chapter 6). Tempting as this beach looks, it is not advisable to swim here because the waves are powerful and tricky. The steady winds make Sandy Beach a popular place to fly kites. From here the road twists and turns next to steep cliffs along the Koko Head shoreline.

Offshore, the islands of Moloka'i and Lāna'i call like distant sirens, and every once in a while, Maui is visible in blue silhouette. For the best photos, pull into the parking lot at **Hālona Blowhole** ㊵. At the top of the hill on the makai side of the road is the entrance to **Hanauma Bay** ㊶, a marine conservation district and the island's premier snorkeling spot.

From here back to Waikīkī the highway passes several residential communities called Hawai'i Kai, Niu Valley, and 'Āina Haina, each of which has a small shopping center with a food store if you need a soda or a snack. Best to keep driving, however, because during rush hour Kalaniana'ole Highway becomes choked with commuter traffic.

Right before you turn off from Kalaniana'ole Highway you'll notice a long stretch of green on the makai side. This is the private Wai'alae Country Club, scene of the televised annual Hawaiian Open Golf Tournament (☞ Spectator Sports *in* Chapter 6).

Take the Kāhala exit. Turn left at the stoplight onto Kīlauea Avenue. Here you'll see Kāhala Mall (☞ Shopping Centers *in* Chapter 7), an upscale shopping complex with yuppie eateries, high-fashion stores, and eight movie theaters. A few blocks past the mall, take a left on Hunakai Street and follow it until it dead-ends at Kāhala Avenue. Turn right and drive through **Kāhala** ㊷, O'ahu's wealthiest neighborhood.

Kāhala Avenue becomes Diamond Head Road; follow it straight to Kapi'olani Park. Stay on the right side of the park until you hit Kapahulu Avenue. Take a left, and you're back in Waikīkī.

TIMING

If Hanauma Bay is your main focus, avoid Wednesday, when hours are limited. Also note that the bay is best in the early hours before the waters are churned up. You could reverse the above directions and get there first thing in the morning, before the crowds. Allow two hours for Hanauma Bay, two hours for Sea Life Park, and one for Queen Emma Summer Palace. Another tip: Look up to the top of the mountains and, if it's clear, head directly to the Pali Lookout; it's a shame to get there only to find the view obscured by clouds or fog. Bring a jacket along; temperatures at the summit are several degrees cooler than in warm Waikīkī.

Take your time, take all day, and enjoy a few beaches along the way. The weather is sunny and warm year-round, and the scenery of O'ahu's east side is too miraculous to rush through.

Sights to See

㊵ **Hālona Blowhole.** Below a scenic turnout along the Koko Head shoreline, this well-photographed lava tube that sucks the ocean in and spits it out in lofty plumes may or may not perform, depending on the currents. Nearby is the tiny beach used to film the wave-washed love scene in

From Here to Eternity. As you face the blowhole and the ocean, look down to your right to see the beach. A rough, steep trail leads to the beach, which is pretty but not recommended for swimming or even wading. Lock your car, because the spot is frequented by thieves. ⊠ *Kalaniana'ole Hwy., 1 mi east of Hanauma Bay.*

🐚 ④① **Hanauma Bay.** If you make only one stop during your drive, this should be it. Even from the overlook, the horseshoe-shape bay is a beauty, and you can easily see the reefs through the clear aqua waters. You can also see the crowds of people snorkeling and sunbathing, but it's still worth a visit to this marine conservation district. ⊠ *7455 Kalaniana'ole Hwy.,* ☎ *808/396–4229.* 🖼 *Donation $3; parking $1; mask, fins, and snorkel rental $6.* 🕙 *Thurs.–Tues. 6 AM–7 PM, Wed. noon–7.*

④② **Kāhala.** O'ahu's wealthiest neighborhood has streets lined with multimillion-dollar homes, and the classy **Kāhala Mandarin Oriental Hotel** attracts a prestigious clientele. At intervals along tree-lined Kāhala Avenue are narrow lanes that provide public access to **Kāhala Beach.** ⊠ *East of Diamond Head.*

③⑨ **Makapu'u Point.** This spot has breathtaking views of the ocean, mountains, and the windward islands. The peninsula jutting out in the distance is **Mōkapu,** site of a U.S. Marine base. The spired mountain peak is **Mt. Olomana.** In front of you on the long pier is part of the **Makai Undersea Test Range,** a research facility that is closed to the public. Offshore is **Rabbit Island,** a picturesque cay so named because some think it looks like a swimming bunny.

Nestled in the cliff face is the **Makapu'u Lighthouse,** which is closed to the public. Near the Makapu'u Point turnout, however, you'll find the start of a mile-long paved road (closed to traffic). Hike up it to the top of the 647-ft bluff for a closer view of the lighthouse. ⊠ *Kalaniana'ole Hwy., turnout above Makapu'u Beach.*

③⑤ **Nu'uanu Pali Lookout.** This panoramic perch looks out to windward O'ahu. It was in this region that King Kamehameha I drove defending forces over the edges of the 1,000-ft-high cliffs, thus winning the decisive battle for control of O'ahu. Lock your car if you get out, because break-ins have occurred here. ⊠ *Top of Pali Hwy.*

㉞ Queen Emma Summer Palace. Built in 1848, this stately white home was used by Queen Emma and her family as a retreat from the rigors of court life in hot and dusty Honolulu during the mid-1800s. It contains many excellent examples of Hawaiian quilts and koa furniture of the period, as well as the queen's wedding dress and shoes. ⊠ *2913 Pali Hwy.,* ☎ *808/595–3167.* ☜ *$5.* ☉ *Guided tour daily 9–4.*

OFF THE
BEATEN
PATH

ARIZONA MEMORIAL – A simple, gleaming white structure shields the hulk of the USS *Arizona,* which sank with 1,102 men aboard when the Japanese attacked Pearl Harbor on December 7, 1941. The tour includes a 20-minute documentary and a shuttle-boat ride to the memorial. Appropriate dress is required (no bathing suits or bare feet). Nearby is the USS *Bowfin*.

The USS *Missouri* arrived in Pearl Harbor in 1998 and will open as a memorial museum in the first quarter of 1999. The public will have access to the historic battleship and an adjoining visitor center with educational exhibits. The admission fee will probably be $9. ⊠ *USS Arizona Memorial and Visitor Center, National Park Service, Pearl Harbor,* ☎ *808/422–0561.* ☜ *Free. Tour tickets distributed on a first-come first-served basis, with 1- to 3-hr waits common.* ☉ *Daily 8–3.*

☝ ㊳ Sea Life Park. Dolphins leap and spin, penguins frolic, and a killer whale performs impressive tricks at the shows in this marine life attraction. There's also a 300,000-gallon Hawaiian reef tank where you can come nose-to-nose with hundreds of marine creatures. The Pacific Whaling Museum teaches you about the fascinating history of whaling in Hawai'i. Even if you've seen trained cetaceans at other marine parks, the distinctively Hawaiian flavor makes this place special. The setting alone, right across from the ocean, is worth the price of admission. ⊠ *Kalaniana'ole Hwy., Waimānalo,* ☎ *808/259–7933.* ☜ *$19.95.* ☉ *Daily 9:30–5.*

㊱ Ulupō Heiau. Though they may look like piles of rocks to the uninitiated, *heiau* are sacred stone platforms for the worship of the gods and date to ancient times. *Ulupō* means "night inspiration," referring to the legendary *menehune*, a mythical race of diminutive people, who supposedly built the heiau under the cloak of darkness. ✉ *Behind YMCA at Kalaniana'ole Hwy. and Kailua Rd.*

OFF THE
BEATEN
PATH

POLYNESIAN CULTURAL CENTER – Re-created villages represent Hawai'i, Tahiti, Samoa, Fiji, the Marquesas, New Zealand, and Tonga. Shows and demonstrations enliven the area, and there's a spectacular IMAX film about the sea. Its expansive open-air shopping village features Polynesian handicrafts that are good for souvenirs. If you're staying in Honolulu, it's better to see the center as part of a van tour, so you won't have to drive home after the overwhelming two-hour evening show. Various packages are available, from basic admission with no transportation to an all-inclusive deal. ✉ *55-370 Kamehameha Hwy., Lā'ie,* ☎ *808/293–3333 or 808/923–1861.* ✆ *$27–$95.* ☉ *Mon.–Sat. 12:30–9.*

37 Waimānalo. This modest little seaside town flanked by chiseled cliffs is worth a visit. Its biggest draw is its beautiful beach, offering glorious views to the windward side. Down the side roads, heading mauka, are little farms that grow a variety of fruits and flowers. Toward the back of the valley are small ranches with grazing horses. If you see any trucks selling corn and you're staying at a place where you can cook it, be sure to get some in Waimānalo. It may be the sweetest you'll ever eat, and the price is the lowest on O'ahu. ✉ *Kalaniana'ole Hwy.*

3 Dining

Updated
by Marty
Wentzel

THE STRENGTH OF HAWAII'S tourist industry has allowed O'ahu's hotels to attract and pay for some of the best culinary talent in the world. However, more and more former hotel chefs have started their own restaurants, which is good news for diners who want fine food, but don't want to pay the generally high hotel restaurant prices.

O'ahu's cuisines are as complex as its population, with Asian, European, and Pacific flavors most prevalent. So pervasive is the Eastern influence that even the McDonald's menu is posted in both English and *kanji,* the universal script of the Orient. In addition to its regular fare, McDonald's serves saimin, a Japanese noodle soup that ranks as the local favorite snack. Thai and Vietnamese cuisines are also local mainstays.

In addition you'll find influences from such far-flung destinations as Mexico and Turkey as well as the staples of the Hawaiian diet. Honolulu is much, but not all, of the O'ahu dining scene. As you head away from town there are a handful of culinary gems, which are often less expensive than the city restaurants.

These days, many of Honolulu's successful restaurants are serving Contemporary fare. Some chefs call it Hawai'i Regional, others Euro-Asian, and still others Pacific Rim, but by any name, this cutting-edge cuisine focuses on the use of Hawai'i's products to keep flavors fresh and island-inspired.

For snacks and fast food around the island, look for the *manapua* wagons, the food trucks usually parked at beaches, and *okazuya* stores, the local version of delis, which dispense tempura, sushi, and plate lunch, Hawai'i's unofficial state dish. A standard plate lunch has macaroni salad, "two scoop rice," and an entrée that might be curry stew, *kālua* (roasted) pork and cabbage, or sweet-and-sour spareribs.

CATEGORY	COST*
$$$$	over $60
$$$	$40–$60
$$	$20–$40
$	under $20

per person for a three-course meal, excluding drinks, service, and 4.17% sales tax

Waikīkī

Chinese

$$–$$$ **✕ Golden Dragon.** A tasty bill of fare focuses primarily on
★ Cantonese and unconventional nouvelle-Chinese cuisine, prepared and served by chef Steve Chiang to his rigorously maintained high standards of excellence. The restaurant has a stunning red-and-black color scheme, and there are big lazy Susans on each table for easy sampling of your companion's menu choices. Signature dishes include stir-fried lobster, and Szechuan beef. Peking duck and beggar's chicken (whole chicken wrapped in lotus leaves and baked in a clay pot) must be ordered 24 hours in advance. ⊠ *Hilton Hawaiian Village, 2005 Kālia Rd.,* ☎ *808/946–5336. Reservations essential. AE, D, DC, MC, V. No lunch.*

Contemporary

$$$– **✕ Orchids.** Flavors from the East and West intermingle on
$$$$ the Orchids menu. Dubbed Indo-Pacific cuisine, the dishes
★ here focus on combinations of Asian spices and herbs in Western-style preparations. For instance, the Peking chive poi crepe is filled with spiny Hawaiian lobster, Chinese greens, and spicy tomato coulis. The duck leg confit with Asian spices comes with sautéed spinach and wild mushrooms. You can't beat the setting right beside the sea, with Diamond Head in the distance and fresh orchids everywhere. Outdoor and indoor seating is available, with the best views from the lānai. The popular Sunday brunch has table after table of all-you-can-eat delights. ⊠ *Halekūlani, 2199 Kālia Rd.,* ☎ *808/923–2311. Reservations essential. AE, MC, V.*

$$$ **✕ Bali by the Sea.** Like the island it's named for, this
★ restaurant is breeze-swept and pretty, with an oceanside setting offering glorious views of Waikīkī Beach. But don't be fooled by the name. This is not a Polynesian eatery but an

internationally acclaimed restaurant featuring such entrées as roast duck with black currant and litchi glaze. Another favorite is the *kiawe 'ōpakapaka* (mesquite-broiled red snapper) with shiitake and asparagus risotto. American pastry chef Gale O'Malley is so talented that he has been decorated by the French government, and the sommelier is one of the wisest and wittiest in Waikīkī. ⊠ *Hilton Hawaiian Village, 2005 Kālia Rd.,* ☎ *808/941–2254. Reservations essential. AE, D, DC, MC, V. No dinner Sun.*

$$–$$$ ✕ **Cascada.** This Waikīkī gem is surprisingly serene, considering it's right next to the lobby of its host hotel. The dining room has warm yellow walls, a hand-painted trompe l'oeil ceiling, and ceramic wall panels. Tables spill out onto an outer marble terrace with tropical gardens and a cascading waterfall. Cuisines of France, Italy, and California are all in evidence in such entrées as scallops topped with an orange-pomegranate butter sauce, roast duck with sweet-sour cherry sauce, and sautéed veal with a compote of Maui onions and tamarind and port wine sauce. ⊠ *Royal Garden at Waikīkī, 440 'Olohana St.,* ☎ *808/943–0202. AE, D, DC, MC, V.*

$$–$$$ ✕ **Hau Tree Lānai.** This restaurant right beside the sand at Kaimana Beach is often overlooked, but it shouldn't be. At breakfast, lunch, or dinner, you can dine under graceful hau trees and hear the whisper of the waves. Breakfast offerings include a huge helping of eggs Benedict, a fluffy Belgian waffle with your choice of toppings (strawberries, bananas, or macadamia nuts), and a tasty fresh salmon omelet. Two standout dinner entrées are the jumbo shrimp with mushrooms, tomatoes, Maui onions, and white wine over fettuccine, and a blue cheese–and–herb crusted New York steak. Romantic torchlight makes this a great place to toast your love. ⊠ *New Otani Kaimana Beach Hotel, 2863 Kalākaua Ave.,* ☎ *808/921–7066. Reservations essential. AE, D, DC, MC, V.*

$$–$$$ ✕ **House Without a Key.** One of the jewels of Waikīkī, this casual seaside spot serves salads, sandwiches, and hearty meals. Special meat, fish, pasta, and chicken entrées are available for lunch or dinner. Favorites include Joy's Sandwich (crabmeat salad, bacon, and avocado on whole-wheat bread) and the beef burger on a kaiser roll. With the ocean and Diamond Head in view, this is a mesmerizing place at sunset,

In case you want to see the world.

At American Express, we're here to make your journey a smooth one. So we have over 1,700 travel service locations in over 120 countries ready to help. What else would you expect from the world's largest travel agency?

do more ®

AMERICAN EXPRESS

Travel

http://www.americanexpress.com/travel

In case you want to be welcomed there.

We're here to see that you're always welcomed at establishments everywhere. That's why millions of people carry the American Express® Card — for peace of mind, confidence, and security, around the world or just around the corner.

do more ®

AMERICAN
EXPRESS

Cards

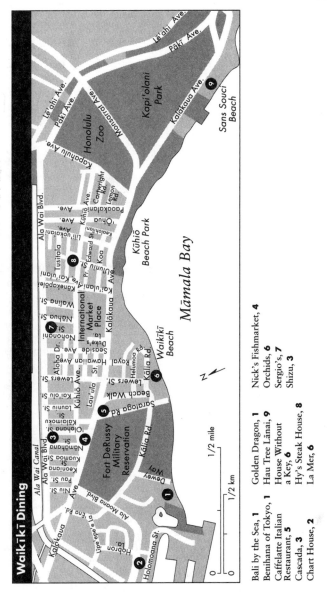

Waikīkī Dining

Bali by the Sea, **1**
Benihana of Tokyo, **1**
Caffelatte Italian Restaurant, **5**
Cascada, **3**
Chart House, **2**
Golden Dragon, **1**
Hau Tree Lānai, **9**
House Without a Key, **6**
Hy's Steak House, **8**
La Mer, **6**
Nick's Fishmarket, **4**
Orchids, **6**
Sergio's, **7**
Shizu, **3**

when there's wonderful live entertainment. A breakfast buffet is served daily 7–10:30. ⊠ *Halekūlani, 2199 Kālia Rd.,* ☏ *808/923–2311. Reservations not accepted. AE, MC, V.*

French

$$$–
$$$$
★

✕ **La Mer.** In the exotic, oceanfront atmosphere of a Mandalay mansion, you'll be served neoclassic French cuisine that many consider to be the finest dining in Hawai'i. Portions are beautifully presented. A standout among the entrées is *onaga* (snapper) fillet cooked skin side crisp with confit of tomato, truffle juice, and fried basil. A favorite sweet is the symphony of four desserts. Each evening there are two complete dinner menus: four courses for $89 and six courses for $105. Highly recommended is the cheese and port course, offered in lieu of dessert. ⊠ *Halekūlani, 2199 Kālia Rd.,* ☏ *808/923–2311. Reservations essential. Jacket required. AE, MC, V. No lunch.*

Italian

$$–$$$$

✕ **Sergio's.** Started in 1976 by the late Sergio Battistetti, this popular dining room offers a tantalizing taste of Italy in the heart of Waikīkī. The atmosphere is sophisticated and romantic, with dark leather booths providing plenty of intimacy. Watch out: Appetizers like baby artichokes dipped in marinara sauce are so good they can ruin your appetite for dinner. Among the pasta dishes is the *bugili puttanesca*, whose wide noodles swim in a tomato sauce spiced by anchovies and capers. Other fine entrées include fettuccine *fruitti di mare* with shrimp, scallops, mussels, and calamari. The wine list is extensive and well thought out. ⊠ *'Ilima Hotel, 445 Nohonani St.,* ☏ *808/926–3388. MC, V.*

$$$

✕ **Caffelatte Italian Restaurant.** There are only three restaurants in Honolulu run by native Italians, and this is one of them. A family from Milan operates this tiny trattoria with limited seating inside and a few tables outside on the narrow lānai. Every dish is worth ordering, from the gnocchi in a thick, rich sauce of Gorgonzola cheese, to the veal scallopini in a light white wine sauce sprinkled with parsley. For dessert, the tiramisu (an airy mocha-and-mascarpone trifle) is the best in town. Be aware that each person must order three courses (appetizer, main course, and dessert), a rule that keeps the tab on the high side. The chef will prepare a special mystery dinner for two for $60. There's no parking, so walk here if you can. ⊠ *339 Saratoga Rd., 2nd level,* ☏ *808/924–1414. AE, DC, MC, V. Closed Tues.*

Japanese

$$-$$$ ✕ **Shizu.** Looking out to an extensive Japanese rock garden, this 40-seat dining room has marble floors and walls, beige and black-lacquer tables and chairs, and etched-glass partitions. The two teppanyaki rooms, which seat 8 and 10 people respectively, have spectacular stained-glass windows with vibrant irises. Teppanyaki diners sit around a massive iron grill on which a dexterous chef slices and cooks sizzling meats and vegetables, served with rice. Traditional Japanese cuisine ranges from sashimi, sushi, and tempura to an elaborate 10-course teppanyaki dinner. Try green-tea cheesecake for dessert. ⊠ *Royal Garden at Waikīkī, 440 'Olohana St., 4th floor,* ☏ *808/943–0202. AE, D, DC, MC, V.*

$-$$ ✕ **Benihana of Tokyo.** These restaurants are as famous for their cutting-board theatrics at the *teppan* (iron grill) tables as they are for their food. You are seated at a long table with other diners, to watch as steak, chicken, seafood, and a variety of vegetables are sliced, diced, tossed, and sautéed before your eyes. There's not much variety to the menu, but it's still a lot of fun. Finish off the meal with some green-tea ice cream, a Benihana tradition. ⊠ *Hilton Hawaiian Village, 2005 Kālia Rd.,* ☏ *808/955–5955. Reservations essential. AE, D, DC, MC, V.*

Seafood

$$-$$$$ ✕ **Chart House.** You can overlook Ala Wai Yacht Harbor from this popular cocktail spot's second-floor location. (Salty dogs may want to visit Yacht Harbor Pub first, just to the right and below Chart House, where sailors of all sorts gather to quaff a few and swap tales.) The decor ranges from varnished wood to saltwater aquariums, glass fishing floats to racing sailboat photos. Dinner specialties include Hawaiian lobster and other seafood, as well as steak. The Dungeness crab is quite good. ⊠ *'Ilikai Waikīkī Hotel, Marina Bldg., 1765 Ala Moana Blvd.,* ☏ *808/941–6669. AE, D, DC, MC, V.*

$$-$$$$ ✕ **Nick's Fishmarket.** It's a little old-fashioned, perhaps—
★ black booths, candlelight, and formal table settings—but for seafood, it's hard to beat Nick's. The bouillabaisse is

an outstanding combination of lobster, crab, prawns, mussels, clams, and fish. Nick's is one of the few places with abalone on the menu; here it's sautéed and served with lobster risotto. Leave room for vanbana pie, a decadent combination of bananas, vanilla Swiss almond ice cream, and hot caramel sauce. ⊠ *Waikīkī Gateway Hotel, 2070 Kalākaua Ave.,* ☎ *808/955–6333. Reservations essential. AE, D, DC, MC, V.*

Steak

$$–$$$$ ✕ **Hy's Steak House.** Things always seem to go well at Hy's, from the filet mignon tartare and oysters Rockefeller right through to the flaming desserts, such as cherries jubilee. The atmosphere is snug and librarylike, and you can watch the chef perform behind glass. Tuxedoed waiters, catering to your every need, make helpful suggestions about the menu. Hy's is famous for its *kiawe*-broiled New York strip steak (kiawe is a mesquite-type wood), peppercorn steak, and rack of lamb. The Caesar salad is excellent, as are the panfried O'Brien potatoes. ⊠ *Waikīkī Park Heights Hotel, 2440 Kūhiō Ave.,* ☎ *808/922–5555. Reservations essential. AE, DC, MC, V. No lunch.*

Honolulu

American/Casual

$–$$ ✕ **California Pizza Kitchen.** This pair of dining and watering holes for young fast-trackers is worth the more-than-likely wait for a table. At the Kāhala site, a glass atrium with tiled and mirrored walls and one side open to the shopping mall creates a sidewalk-café effect. The pizzas have toppings you'd never expect, such as Thai chicken, Peking duck, and Caribbean shrimp. The pastas, made fresh daily on the premises, include angel hair, fettuccine, rigatoni, fusilli, and linguine. ⊠ *Kāhala Mall, 4211 Wai'alae Ave.,* ☎ *808/ 737–9446;* ⊠ *1910 Ala Moana Blvd., Waikīkī,* ☎ *808/955– 5161. Reservations not accepted. AE, D, DC, MC, V.*

$–$$ ✕ **Hard Rock Cafe.** The Honolulu branch of this international chain has rock-and-roll memorabilia along with surfboards and aloha shirts for local color. The Hard Rock has always sold more T-shirts than T-bones, so don't expect any culinary surprises on its formula menu. The portion-controlled quarter-pound burgers hold sway, but don't overlook the 'ahi steak sandwiches or baby back ribs as alternatives. French fries are, of course, a must with any choice. The decibel level of the oldies playing over the sound system is set at "too loud," and you'll probably have to wait for a table. ⊠ *1837 Kapi'olani Blvd.,* ☎ *808/ 955–7583. Reservations not accepted. AE, MC, V.*

Barbecue

$–$$ ✗ **Dixie Grill.** This Southern-inspired eatery emphasizes just how much fun food can be. Why, there's even an outdoor sandbox for the kids! Dixie Grill specializes in baby back ribs, smoked barbecue chicken, whole Dungeness crab, campfire steak, and fried catfish. Recipes for the barbecue sauces come from Memphis, the Carolinas, Georgia, and Texas. Sandwiches, salads, and comfort foods like meat loaf round out the dinner menu. Save room for the Georgia peach cobbler. ⊠ *404 Ward Ave.,* ☎ *808/596– 8359. AE, D, DC, MC, V.*

Chinese

$–$$ ✗ **Maple Garden.** The fine reputation of Maple Garden is founded on spicy Mandarin cuisine, not on decor. There are some booths, some tables, an Oriental screen or two, and lights that are a little too bright at times. It's comfortable, however, and that's all that matters, because the food is delicious. A consistent favorite is the eggplant in a tantalizing hot garlic sauce. ⊠ *909 Isenberg St.,* ☎ *808/941–6641. MC, V.*

Contemporary

$$–$$$ ✗ **Alan Wong's.** Wong focuses heavily on Hawaiian-grown
★ products to keep the flavors super-fresh, and he's utterly creative, turning local "grinds" into gourmet treats. For starters, get "Da Bag," a puffed-up foil bag that's punctured at the table, revealing steamed clams, *kālua* pork, spinach, and shiitake mushrooms. Garlic-mashed potatoes come with a black bean salsa, grilled pork chops with a coconut-ginger sweet potato puree. The low-key dining room has a display kitchen, while the enclosed *lānai* serves up views of the Ko'olau Mountains. Don't miss the coconut sorbet served in a chocolate–and–macadamia nut shell, surrounded by exotic fruits. Finding the restaurant can be dif-

ficult: Look for a white apartment building and a small sign after a parking garage, where your car can be valet parked. ⊠ *McCully Court, 1857 S. King St., 3rd floor,* ☎ *808/949–2526. AE, MC, V. No lunch.*

$$–$$$ ✕ **Hoku's.** Wall-to-wall ocean views, a gleaming kitchen visible to diners, and an oyster and sushi bar vie for attention at this multilevel restaurant, the Kāhala Mandarin's signature dining room. Asian, Mediterranean, and French cuisines command the menu. You might choose an appetizer of Peking duck spring rolls with mango, sunflower sprouts, and hoisin sauce. Entrées range from roast chicken with bok choy to bouillabaisse with lobster, prawns, scallops, and clams. Be sure to sample naan bread from the tandoori oven. ⊠ *Kāhala Mandarin Oriental Hawai'i, 5000 Kāhala Ave.,* ☎ *808/739–8888. AE, DC, MC, V.*

$$–$$$ ✕ **Kāhala Moon.** Koa furnishings, brocade upholstery, and
★ local art set the tone at this pretty restaurant in one of Honolulu's most upscale neighborhoods. Local ingredients pervade the menu, from Waimānalo greens to kukui nut salad dressing. Start with the meaty portobello mushrooms on French bread in a demi-glace. As a main dish, try the fillet of snapper on a bed of julienned zucchini and carrots. When banana soufflé with chocolate sauce is offered, don't hesitate to order it. ⊠ *4614 Kīlauea Ave.,* ☎ *808/732–7777. AE, DC, MC, V.*

$$–$$$ ✕ **Sam Choy's.** His motto is "Never trust a skinny chef,"
★ and indeed, Choy's broad girth and even broader smile let you know you'll be well taken care of here. The theme is upscale local, as the Hawai'i-born chef contemporizes the foods he grew up with. The result? Brie-stuffed wontons with pineapple marmalade, fresh fish and vegetables wrapped in ti leaves, seared 'ahi seasoned with ginger, and roasted duck with a Big Island orange sauce. Portions are huge; two people can easily split an entrée. ⊠ *449 Kapahulu Ave., 2nd level,* ☎ *808/732–8645. AE, MC, V. No lunch.*

$$–$$$ ✕ **Sunset Grill.** The sweet smell of wood smoke greets you as you enter the Sunset Grill, which specializes in *kiawe*-broiled foods. The place is supposed to feel unfinished, with the marble bar top and white tablecloths contrasting nicely with the concrete floors. The *salade niçoise,* big enough for a whole dinner, includes red-top lettuce, beans, tomato, egg, potatoes, and olives, with marinated grilled 'ahi. The trout and scallops, cooked in a wood oven, are both very good, and the daily specials, especially the pastas, are always worth a try. ⊠ *Restaurant Row, 500 Ala Moana Blvd.,* ☎ *808/521–4409. AE, DC, MC, V.*

$$–$$$ ✕ **3660 On The Rise.** This stellar eatery is a 10-minute drive
★ from Waikīkī, in the up-and-coming culinary mecca of Kaimukī. Light hardwoods, frosted glass, green marble, and black granite mix in a leisurely fashion here, and there's almost always a full house in the 90-seat dining room (with room for 20 on a streetside lānai outside). Homegrown ingredients are combined with European flavors: Dungeness crab cakes are prepared in a nest of angel hair and served with a ginger-cilantro aioli, and fettuccine is topped with assorted sautéed shellfish and grilled shiitake mushrooms. For dessert, try the warm chocolate soufflé cake with espresso sauce and vanilla ice cream. ⊠ *3660 Wai'alae Ave.,* ☎ *808/737–1177. AE, DC, MC, V.*

$–$$$ ✕ **Palomino.** At the top of a grand staircase, lavish Palomino
★ has handblown glass chandeliers, hand-painted roses, American and African woods, and a 50-ft marble and mahogany bar. Entrées from the wood-burning oven include mahimahi with creamy polenta, fig-caper-olive relish, and mussels. For seafood, order the crab cakes with pesto beurre blanc; if pasta is your preference, go for the fusilli with hot Portuguese sausage. This restaurant is close to downtown's Hawai'i Theatre. From Aloha Tower Marketplace, look for it across Ala Moana Boulevard. ⊠ *Harbor Court, 66 Queen St., 3rd floor,* ☎ *808/528–2400. AE, D, DC, MC, V.*

$$ ✕ **Indigo.** Local boy Glenn Chu turned Honolulu on its ear
★ by daring to open a trendy restaurant in a seedy downtown neighborhood—and succeeding. The decor emphasizes wicker and track lighting, with a charming back lānai that shields you from the downtown hubbub. Marrying East with West, Chu's variations on foods from his Chinese heritage include crispy wontons stuffed with hot goat cheese, Szechuan peppered beef loin in black bean sauce, and prawns with hot chili-garlic sauce. ⊠ *1121 Nu'uanu Ave.,* ☎ *808/521–2900. AE, D, DC, MC, V.*

$$ ✕ **A Pacific Café O'ahu.** Take Asian, Mediterranean, and
★ Indian cuisines and combine them with a love of Hawai'i's homegrown products. The result: Chef Jean-Marie Josselin's award-winning menu, a true O'ahu standout. Lunch

highlights include a mixed green salad with grilled Japanese eggplant, goat cheese, and chili vinaigrette; and a shiitake mushroom sandwich with mozzarella. At dinner the wok-charred mahimahi with a garlic, sesame crust, and lime-ginger beurre blanc is superb. The interior—designed by Josselin's wife, Sophronia—is at once whimsical, sophisticated, and modern. ⊠ *Ward Centre, 1200 Ala Moana Blvd.,* ☎ *808/593–0035. AE, DC, MC, V.*

$–$$ ✕ **Gordon Biersch Brewery Restaurant.** Snuggling up to
★ Honolulu Harbor, this indoor-outdoor eatery, part of a West Coast–based chain of microbreweries, is Aloha Tower Marketplace's busiest. The menu is American with an Island twist, from chicken skewers in a hot peanut-coconut sauce to fresh-seared *'ahi* in a *sansho* (tuna in a Japanese pepper) crust, plus a variety of pastas and pizzas. You can smell the garlic fries the moment you walk in. All that spicy food goes well with the beer, which is made on the premises. Ask for tastes of the dark, medium, and light brews before choosing your favorite. ⊠ *Aloha Tower Marketplace, 101 Ala Moana Blvd.,* ☎ *808/599–4877. AE, D, DC, MC, V.*

$ ✕ **Kaka'ako Kitchen.** The floors are concrete, the furniture is plastic, and the plates are Styrofoam. Never mind; this is the place to go for a healthy plate lunch (previously a contradiction in terms). In a converted warehouse, the kitchen turns out local favorites like pan-seared chicken salad, teriyaki chicken sandwich, and sautéed mahimahi. You can even order brown rice and a side of mesclun greens. ⊠ *1216 Waimanu St.,* ☎ *808/594–3663. Reservations not accepted. No credit cards. No dinner Sat.–Tues.*

German

$ ✕ **Patisserie.** By day, this bakery is dominated by fluorescent lights and a shining display case, but five nights a week it turns into a 24-seat restaurant with great German food, a rarity in Hawai'i. The menu is small, with 10 entrées, but any choice is a good choice. The Wiener schnitzel is juicy within its crispy crust, and veal ribs are garnished with a sprig of rosemary. Try the potato pancakes, crisp outside and soft inside, joined by a healthy spoonful of applesauce. Tossed salad and European-style breads are included in the price. The single dessert is apple strudel, standing high and full of rum-soaked raisins and tart apples and served on a rich sauce of cream, egg yolks, and vanilla beans. ⊠ *Kāhala*

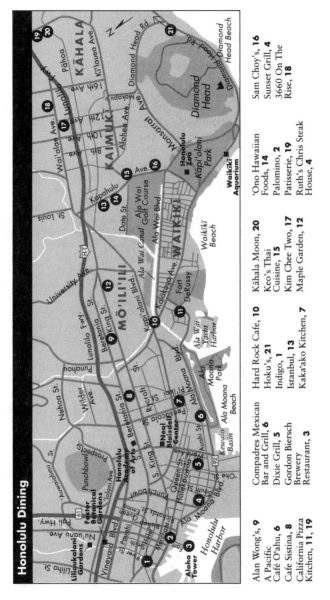

Honolulu Dining

Alan Wong's, **9**

A Pacific
Café O'ahu, **6**

Café Sistina, **8**

California Pizza
Kitchen, **11**, **19**

Compadres Mexican
Bar and Grill, **6**

Dixie Grill, **5**

Gordon Biersch
Brewery
Restaurant, **3**

Hard Rock Cafe, **10**

Hoku's, **21**

Indigo, **1**

Istanbul, **13**

Kaka'ako Kitchen, **7**

Kahala Moon, **20**

Keo's Thai
Cuisine, **15**

Kim Chee Two, **17**

Maple Garden, **12**

'Ono Hawaiian
Foods, **14**

Palomino, **2**

Patisserie, **19**

Ruth's Chris Steak
House, **4**

Sam Choy's, **16**

Sunset Grill, **4**

3660 On The
Rise, **18**

Mall, 4211 Wai'alae Ave., ☎ *808/735–4402. Reservations not accepted. MC, V. BYOB. Closed Sun.–Mon.*

Hawaiian

$ ✕ **'Ono Hawaiian Foods.** Locals frequent this no-frills hangout for a regular hit of their favorite foods. You can tell it's good, because there's usually a line outside after about 5 PM. In a plain storefront site and furnished simply with tables and booths, this small (it seats about 40) restaurant is a good place to do some taste testing of such Island innovations as poi, *lomilomi* salmon (salmon massaged until tender and served with minced onions and tomatoes), *laulau* (steamed bundle of ti leaves containing pork, butterfish, and taro tops), *kālua* pork, and *haupia* (a light, gelatinlike dessert made from coconut). Appropriately enough, the Hawaiian word *'ono* means delicious. ⊠ *726 Kapahulu Ave.,* ☎ *808/737–2275. Reservations not accepted. No credit cards. Closed Sun.*

Italian

$–$$ ✕ **Cafe Sistina.** Sergio Mitrotti has gained quite a following with his inventive Italian-Mediterranean cuisine. He's concocted an appetizer of goat cheese, chili peppers, garlic, prosciutto, and Greek olives, and he fills ravioli with such delights as Gorgonzola, porcini mushrooms, red peppers, and pancetta cream. Linguine *alla puttanesca* comes alive with tomatoes, onions, capers, and kalamata olives. Fresh chewy bread comes with a pesto butter to die for. A graphic artist by training, Mitrotti has painted the café's walls with Italianesque scenes. ⊠ *1314 S. King St.,* ☎ *808/ 596–0061. AE, MC, V.*

Korean

$ ✕ **Kim Chee Two.** Here's an unassuming little carry-out and sit-down restaurant featuring Korean food. The prices are low and the portions are big, and you get little side dishes of spicy *kimchi* (a fiery pickled Korean condiment) with your meal. This is a fun place to try such specialties as *bi bim kook soo* (noodles with meat and vegetables), meat *jun* (barbecued beef coated with egg and highly seasoned), *chop chae* (fried vegetables and noodles), and fried *man doo* (plump meat-filled dumplings). ⊠ *3569 Wai'alae Ave.,* ☎ *808/737–0006. Reservations not accepted. No credit cards. BYOB.*

Mediterranean

$–$$ ✕ **Istanbul.** Surrounded by tourist posters and serenaded by recorded Turkish music, diners here can encounter the lively flavors of the sunny Mediterranean. Rolled, deep-fried *mezeler* (appetizers) contain combinations of such fillings as feta cheese with parsley and fried eggplant with yogurt. Kebab plates come with beef, lamb, or chicken accompanied by rice and a zesty cucumber-onion-tomato salad with lemon. Depending on your mood, you may or may not want to time your visit with the nightly belly dancing (7:30–8:30). ⊠ *740 Kapahulu Ave.,* ☎ *808/735–6667. AE, MC, V. No lunch.*

Mexican

$–$$ ✕ **Compadres Mexican Bar and Grill.** The after-work crowd gathers here for frosty pitchers of potent margaritas and yummy pūpū. An outdoor terrace with patio-style furnishings is best for cocktails and chips. Inside, the wooden floors, colorful photographs, and lively paintings create a festive setting for imaginative Mexican specialties. Fajitas, baby back ribs, and grilled shrimp are just a few of the many offerings. ⊠ *Ward Centre, 1200 Ala Moana Blvd.,* ☎ *808/ 591–8307. Reservations not accepted. D, MC, V.*

Steak

$$–$$$ ✕ **Ruth's Chris Steak House.** At last, a steak joint that doesn't look like one. This pastel-hued dining room on Restaurant Row caters to meat lovers by serving mouth-watering top-of-the-line steak cuts. The portions are large, so bring an appetite. Side orders include generous salads and an ultra-creamy spinach au gratin. Charbroiled fish, veal, and lamb chops provide tasty alternatives to the steaks. For dessert, try the house special, a bread pudding happily soaked in whisky sauce. ⊠ *Restaurant Row, 500 Ala Moana Ave.,* ☎ *808/599–3860. AE, DC, MC, V.*

Thai

$$ ✕ **Keo's Thai Cuisine.** Hollywood celebrities have discov-
★ ered this twinkling nook with tables set amid lighted trees, big paper umbrellas, and sprays of orchids everywhere. In fact, photos of Keo with different star patrons are displayed on one wall. Favorite dishes include Evil Jungle Prince (shrimp, vegetables, or chicken in a sauce flavored with fresh basil, coconut milk, and red chili) and *chiang*

mai salad (chicken salad seasoned with lemongrass, red chili, mint, and fish sauce). Ask for your food mild or medium; it'll still be hot, but not as hot as it *could* be. For dessert, the apple bananas (small, tart bananas grown in Hawai'i) in coconut milk are wonderful. ⊠ *625 Kapahulu Ave.,* ☎ *808/737–8240. Reservations essential. AE, D, DC, MC, V. No lunch.*

Around the Island

Hawai'i Kai

CONTEMPORARY

$$ ✕ **Roy's.** Two walls of windows offer views of Maunalua Bay and Diamond Head in the distance, and a glassed-in kitchen affords views of what's cooking at Roy Yamaguchi's Hawai'i Kai venture. This is a noisy two-story restaurant with a devoted following; Roy also has branches on the Big Island, Maui, and Kaua'i. The menu matches Hawai'i flavors with Euro-Asian accents. It's hard to find a better blackened 'ahi in a hot, soy-mustard butter sauce. Of the individual pizzas, the best is topped with vine-ripened tomatoes, goat cheese, and roasted garlic. ⊠ *Hawai'i Kai Corporate Plaza, 6600 Kalaniana'ole Hwy.,* ☎ *808/396–7697. AE, D, DC, MC, V.*

Kailua

MEXICAN

$ ✕ **Bueno Nalo.** Long a Waimānalo landmark, this family-run eatery moved to the windward side of the island in 1998. It's still run by the same owners, who are dedicated to healthy Mexican cuisine. Velvet paintings and piñatas add a fun, funky flavor to the setting. The food is reliably good. *Topopo* salad is a heap of greens, tomatoes, onions, tuna, olives, cheese, and beans on top of a tortilla. Combination plates with tacos, enchiladas, and tamales are bargains, and the chili rellenos are expertly seasoned. Families will appreciate the eight-piece Mexican pizzas and the keiki menu for children 10 and under. ⊠ *20 Kainehe St.,* ☎ *808/263–1999. Reservations not accepted for parties of fewer than 6. AE, MC, V.*

4 Lodging

O'AHU HAS A WIDE RANGE OF AC-
COMMODATIONS. First consider
whether your South Seas dream va-
cation includes getting away from the usual hustle and
bustle. If so, consider 'Ihilani Resort & Spa, just a 25-
minute drive from Honolulu International Airport. If you
prefer proximity to the action, go for a hotel or condominium
in or near Waikīkī, where most of the island's lodgings are.

Updated
by Marty
Wentzel

Below is a selective list of lodging choices in each price cat-
egory; for a complete list of every hotel and condominium
on the island, write or call the Hawai'i Visitors and Convention Bureau for a free *Accommodation Guide* (☞ Visitor Information *in* Essential Information). It details amenities
and gives each hotel's proximity to the beach.

CATEGORY	COST*
$$$$	over $200
$$$	$125–$200
$$	$75–$125
$	under $75

*All prices are for a standard double room, excluding
11.41% tax and service charges.

Waikīkī

$$$$ 🏨 **Aston Waikīkī Beach Tower.** Elegance oozes out of this
39-story luxury condominium resort overlooking Waikīkī
Beach. It has stylish one- and two-bedroom suites fitted with
microwaves, dishwashers, wet bars, washer/dryers, and
private lānai. ✉ 2470 Kalākaua Ave., Honolulu, 96815,
☎ 808/926–6400 or 800/922–7866, FAX 808/922–8785.
140 suites. Kitchenettes, pool, sauna, paddle tennis, shuf-
fleboard. AE, D, DC, MC, V.

$$$$ 🏨 **Halekūlani.** Today's sleek, modern, and luxurious
★   Halekūlani was built around the garden lānai and 1931
building of the gracious old Halekūlani Hotel. The tidy mar-
ble-and-wood rooms have accents of white, beige, blue, and
gray. All have lānai, sitting areas, bathrobes, many terrific
toiletries, and dozens of little touches that are sure to please.
The hotel has two of the finest restaurants in Honolulu and

an oceanside pool with a giant orchid mosaic. ✉ *2199 Kālia Rd., Honolulu, 96815,* ☎ *808/923–2311 or 800/367–2343,* ℻ *808/926–8004. 412 rooms, 44 suites. 3 restaurants, 3 bars, refrigerators, pool, exercise room, beach, meeting rooms. AE, DC, MC, V.*

$$$$ 🏨 **Hawai'i Prince Hotel Waikīkī.** In a departure from the traditional Hawaiian motif, the Prince is a sleek high-rise with the sort of sophisticated interior design generally reserved for a city hotel. You know you're in Waikīkī, however, when you look out your window at the Ala Wai Yacht Harbor. Harbor views can also be had from the elegant Prince Court restaurant, while Hakone serves some of the best authentic Japanese food on the island, including a tantalizing 10-course *kaiseki* dinner (a traditional meal of small, artful, bite-size portions). There's a free shuttle to the beach and downtown. ✉ *100 Holomoana St., Honolulu, 96815,* ☎ *808/956–1111 or 800/321–6248,* ℻ *808/946–0811. 467 rooms, 54 suites. 3 restaurants, lobby lounge, pool, meeting rooms. AE, DC, MC, V.*

$$$$ 🏨 **Hilton Hawaiian Village.** Each year Hilton spends a
★   bundle to maintain this lavishly landscaped resort, the largest in Waikīkī. Surrounding its four towers are cascading waterfalls, colorful fish and birds, and even a botanical garden with labeled flora. Rooms are decorated in attractive raspberry or aqua shades, with rattan and bamboo furnishings. The hotel has a dock for its catamaran and a fine stretch of beach. ✉ *2005 Kālia Rd., Honolulu, 96815,* ☎ *808/949–4321 or 800/445–8667,* ℻ *808/947–7898. 2,180 rooms, 365 suites. 6 restaurants, 5 lounges, 3 pools, beach. AE, D, DC, MC, V.*

$$$$ 🏨 **Hyatt Regency Waikīkī.** A 10-story atrium with a two-story waterfall and mammoth metal sculpture, shops, live music, and Harry's Bar make this one of the liveliest lobbies anywhere. The Ciao Mein restaurant serves both Italian and Chinese food. Since the hotel has two towers, there are two Regency Clubs and eight penthouses. Each guest room has a private lānai. The hotel is across from the beach and a short walk from Kapi'olani Park. ✉ *2424 Kalākaua Ave., Honolulu, 96815,* ☎ *808/923–1234 or 800/233–1234,* ℻ *808/923–7839. 1,212 rooms, 18 suites. 4 restaurants, 2 lobby lounges, pool, shops. AE, D, DC, MC, V.*

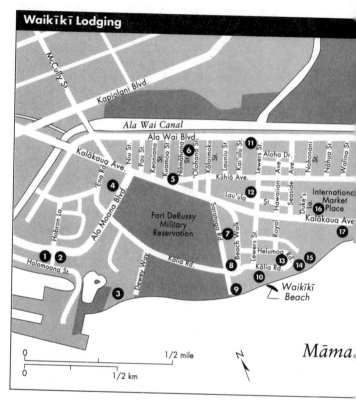

Waikīkī Lodging

Ambassador Hotel, **5**

Aston at the Waikīkī Banyan, **24**

Aston Waikīkī Beach Tower, **25**

Coconut Plaza Hotel, **11**

Continental Surf Hotel, **21**

Doubletree Alana Waikīkī, **4**

Edmunds Hotel Apts., **20**

Halekūlani, **10**

Hawai'i Prince Hotel Waikīkī, **1**

Hawaiian Regent Hotel, **26**

Hawaiian Waikīkī Beach Hotel, **27**

Hilton Hawaiian Village, **3**

Hyatt Regency Waikīkī, **19**

'Ilikai Hotel Nikko Waikīkī, **2**

Malihini Hotel, **7**

New Otani Kaimana Beach Hotel, **29**

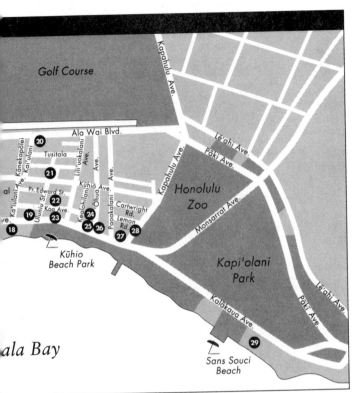

Golf Course

Ala Wai Blvd.

Kapahulu Ave.

Le'ahi Ave.

Pāki Ave.

Tusitala

Kanekapōlei Ave.
Ka'iulani Ave.
Lili'uokalani Ave.
'Ōhua Ave.

Pr. Edward St.
Kūhiō Ave.
Kealohilani Ave.

Ka'iulani Ave.
Uluniu St.
Koa Ave.

Cartwright Rd.
Lemon Rd.
Paoakalani

Honolulu
Zoo

Monsarrat Ave.

Le'ahi Ave.

Pāki Ave.

Kūhio
Beach Park

Kapi'olani
Park

Kalākaua Ave.

ala Bay

Sans Souci
Beach

Outrigger Reef Hotel, **9**	Royal Garden at Waikīkī, **6**	Sheraton Waikīkī, **14**
Outrigger Royal Islander, **8**	Royal Grove Hotel, **22**	Waikīkī Beachcomber Hotel, **16**
Outrigger Waikīkī Hotel, **17**	Royal Hawaiian Hotel, **15**	Waikīkī Hana, **23**
Queen Kapi'olani Hotel, **28**	Sheraton Moana Surfrider, **18**	Waikīkī Joy, **12**
		Waikīkī Parc, **13**

$$$$ ⌧ **ʻIlikai Hotel Nikko Waikīkī.** This is the acknowledged tennis hotel of Waikīkī (courts are on the rooftops) and one of the closest hotels to Ala Moana Shopping Center and Ala Moana Beach Park. There are three towers and a huge esplanade, which is always busy, and crowds gather at sunset for the torch lighting, hula dancing, and live Hawaiian music. ⌧ *1777 Ala Moana Blvd., Honolulu, 96815,* ☎ *808/949–3811 or 800/367–8434,* ℻ *808/947–0892. 728 rooms, 51 suites. 4 restaurants, 2 lobby lounges, 2 pools, 7 tennis courts, meeting rooms. AE, D, DC, MC, V.*

$$$$ ⌧ **Royal Hawaiian Hotel.** This "Pink Palace of the Pacific" was built in 1927, an age of gracious and leisurely
★ travel when people sailed here on luxury liners and spent months in Waikīkī. As befits its era, the hotel has high ceilings, period furniture, and flowered wallpaper. Pink telephones in each room and corridors of pink carpeting add a dreamy quality. The modern wing is more expensive, but for charm—and the tinkle of massive crystal chandeliers—the original building can't be beat. The beachside Mai Tai Bar has views of Diamond Head. ⌧ *2259 Kalākaua Ave., Honolulu, 96815,* ☎ *808/923–7311 or 800/325–3535,* ℻ *808/924–7098. 472 rooms, 53 suites. 3 restaurants, bar, pool, meeting rooms. AE, DC, MC, V.*

$$$$ ⌧ **Sheraton Moana Surfrider.** The Moana Hotel, built in 1901, merged with the newer Surfrider next door. As in the old days, the furnishings on each floor are made of a different kind of wood: mahogany, oak, maple, cherry, and rare Hawaiian koa. The Banyan Court is the focal point for beachfront activity, and you can relax on the gracious veranda, sip tea, and tune yourself in to turn-of-the-century living. ⌧ *2365 Kalākaua Ave., Honolulu, 96815,* ☎ *808/922–3111 or 800/325–3535,* ℻ *808/923–0308. 750 rooms, 41 suites. 3 restaurants, bar, 3 lobby lounges, snack bar, pool, beach, meeting rooms. AE, DC, MC, V.*

$$$$ ⌧ **Sheraton Waikīkī.** The towering Sheraton has spacious rooms, many of which have grand views of Diamond Head. The hotel is just steps away from the multilevel Royal Hawaiian Shopping Center and next to the Royal Hawaiian Hotel. The glass-walled elevator ascends to the Hanohano Room, an elegant dining room with panoramas of the sea and Waikīkī. There's a lounge area with show-

ers for guests who arrive on early flights or leave on late ones. ✉ *2255 Kalākaua Ave., Honolulu, 96815,* ☎ *808/ 922–4422 or 800/325–3535,* FAX *808/922–7708. 1,588 rooms, 131 suites. 5 restaurants, 3 lobby lounges, 2 pools, health club, beach, children's programs, meeting rooms. AE, DC, MC, V.*

$$$– $$$$ 🏨 **Doubletree Alana Waikīkī.** Leisure and business travelers like this hotel's location on the west edge of Waikīkī, two blocks from Ala Moana Shopping Center and Ala Moana Beach Park and 4 mi from downtown Honolulu. Public areas of the 19-story high-rise are modern and attractive, with art exhibits in the lobby. Guest rooms have private lānai with panoramic views of the mountains or ocean. Workaholics will like the 'round-the-clock services of the business center. ✉ *1956 Ala Moana Blvd., Honolulu, 96815,* ☎ *808/941–7275 or 800/367–6070,* FAX *808/949– 0996. 268 rooms, 45 suites. Restaurant, lobby lounge, pool, exercise room, business services. AE, D, MC, V.*

$$$– $$$$ 🏨 **Hawaiian Regent Hotel.** With two towers and two lobbies, this property's layout is a bit confusing, but if you can get past that, this is a decent hotel. The huge lobbies and courtyards open to ocean breezes are sunlit and tropical in feeling. Better yet, it's right across the street from Waikīkī Beach. Several dining choices include two Japanese restaurants and a cutting-edge Mediterranean dining room called Acqua. The shopping arcade has 20 shops and boutiques. ✉ *2552 Kalākaua Ave., Honolulu, 96815,* ☎ *808/922– 6611 or 800/367–5370,* FAX *808/921–5222. 1,337 rooms, 9 suites. 5 restaurants, 2 lobby lounges, 2 pools, tennis court, shops, dance club, meeting rooms. AE, D, MC, V.*

$$$– $$$$ 🏨 **Hawaiian Waikīkī Beach Hotel.** The site—close to Kapi'olani Park, the zoo, and other attractions and across from the beach—is excellent, and the seawall in front of the hotel offers the best sunset views. The mauka tower offers mainly ocean views. The rooms have rattan furniture, right down to the headboards, and each has a private lānai. The Captain's Table serves meals in surroundings modeled after those of old-time luxury liners. ✉ *2570 Kalākaua Ave., Honolulu, 96815,* ☎ *808/922–2511 or 800/877–7666,* FAX *808/923–3656. 673 rooms, 40 suites. 2 restaurants, 3 lobby lounges, pool. AE, D, DC, MC, V.*

$$$–
$$$$
★
 New Otani Kaimana Beach Hotel. Polished to a shine, this hotel is open to the trade winds and furnished with big, comfortable chairs. The ambience is cheerful and charming, and the lobby has a happy, unpretentious feel. Best of all, it's right on the beach at the quiet end of Waikīkī, practically at the foot of Diamond Head. The staff is friendly and helpful. Rooms are smallish but very nicely appointed, with soothing pastel decor and off-white furnishings. Get a room with an ocean view and dine at least once at the Hau Tree Lānai. ⊠ *2863 Kalākaua Ave., Honolulu, 96815,* ☏ *808/923–1555 or 800/356–8264,* ℻ *808/922–9404. 119 rooms, 6 suites. 2 restaurants, lobby lounge, meeting rooms. AE, D, DC, MC, V.*

$$$–
$$$$
 Queen Kapiʻolani Hotel. Built in 1969, this 19-story hotel is at the east edge of Waikīkī, right across from the Honolulu Zoo and Kapiʻolani Park and a half block from the beach. It appeals to those in search of clean, basic accommodations within walking distance of Waikīkī's main attractions. Rooms have refrigerators, and there's a large freshwater swimming pool and sundeck on the third floor. ⊠ *150 Kapahulu Ave., Honolulu, 96815,* ☏ *808/922–1941 or 800/367–5004,* ℻ *808/922–2694. 308 rooms, 7 suites. Refrigerators, 2 restaurants, bar, pool, meeting rooms. AE, D, DC, MC, V.*

$$$–
$$$$
 Waikīkī Joy. This boutique hotel is a lesser-known gem. One tower has all suites, and another has standard hotel rooms. Units have either ocean or partial ocean views; each has a lānai, a whirlpool bath, a deluxe stereo system with Bose speakers, and a control panel by the bed. The location is great, tucked away on a quiet side street yet still close to Waikīkī's dining, shopping, and entertainment. ⊠ *320 Lewers St., Honolulu, 96815,* ☏ *808/923–2300 or 800/922–7866,* ℻ *808/924–4010. 50 rooms, 44 suites. Restaurant, lobby lounge, kitchenettes, pool, sauna. AE, D, DC, MC, V.*

$$$–
$$$$
★
 Waikīkī Parc. Billed as offering affordable luxury, this hotel lives up to its promise in all essentials except its main entrance (down a narrow side street) and location (not on the beach). The lobby is light and airy, with mirrors and pastel tones. Guest rooms are done in cool blues and whites, with lots of rattan. The hotel has a fine Japanese restaurant called Kacho and the lovely Parc Café, known for its reasonably priced all-you-can-eat buffets. ⊠ *2233 Helu-*

moa Rd., Honolulu, 96815, ☎ 808/921–7272 or 800/ 422–0450, ℻ 808/923–1336. 298 rooms. 2 restaurants, in-room safes, refrigerators, pool. AE, D, DC, MC, V.

$$$ 🏨 Aston at the Waikīkī Banyan. Families enjoy this high-rise condominium resort near Diamond Head, one block from Waikīkī Beach and two blocks from the Honolulu Zoo. One-bedroom suites have daily maid service and private lānai. Look for the fishpond in the lobby area. ⊠ *201 'Ōhua Ave., Honolulu, 96815, ☎ 808/922–0555 or 800/ 922–7866, ℻ 808/922–8785. 876 suites. Snack bar, kitchenettes, pool, sauna, tennis court. AE, D, DC, MC, V.*

$$$ 🏨 Outrigger Reef Hotel. The big advantage here is a location right on the beach. There are fashion and souvenir boutiques in the lobby and the rooms are done in soft mauves and pinks, many with lānai. Ask for an ocean view; the other rooms have decidedly less delightful views. ⊠ *2169 Kālia Rd., Honolulu, 96815, ☎ 808/923–3111 or 800/688– 7444, ℻ 808/924–4957. 846 rooms, 39 suites. 2 restaurants, 4 bars, no-smoking rooms, pool, beach, nightclub, meeting rooms. AE, D, DC, MC, V.*

$$$ 🏨 Outrigger Waikīkī Hotel. Outrigger Hotels & Resorts' star property, on Kalākaua Avenue in the heart of the best shopping and dining action, stands next to some of the nicest sands in Waikīkī. Rooms have a Polynesian motif, and each has a lānai. For more than 25 years, the main ballroom has been home to the sizzling Society of Seven and the group's Las Vegas–style production. ⊠ *2335 Kalākaua Ave., Honolulu, 96815, ☎ 808/923–0711 or 800/688–7444, ℻ 800/622–4852. 500 rooms, 30 suites. 6 restaurants, 5 bars, lobby lounge, kitchenettes, pool. AE, D, DC, MC, V.*

$$$ 🏨 Royal Garden at Waikīkī. From the outside, this 25-story hotel looks like your average Waikīkī high-rise. But step inside and it whispers elegance, from the marble and etched glass in the lobby to the genuine graciousness of the staff. Guest rooms have sitting areas, private lānai, and marble and brass baths. There's a free shuttle service to and from Kapi'olani Park, the shopping centers, and duty-free shops. ⊠ *440 'Olohana St., Honolulu, 96815, ☎ 808/943–0202 or 800/367–5666, ℻ 808/946–8777. 202 rooms, 18 suites. 2 restaurants, lobby lounge, in-room safes, kitchenettes, 2 pools, meeting rooms. CP. AE, D, DC, MC, V.*

$$$ ★ 🏨 **Waikīkī Beachcomber Hotel.** With an excellent location right across the street from Waikīkī Beach, it's also a short walk from the Royal Hawaiian Shopping Center and the International Market Place. Rooms have simple rattan furnishings, with a rose, beige, and off-white color scheme and prints by local artists. Rooms have private lānai. The venerable Don Ho and talented ventriloquist Freddie Morris perform here. ⊠ 2300 Kalākaua Ave., Honolulu, 96815, ☎ 808/922–4646 or 800/622–4646, ℻ 808/923–4889. 487 rooms, 7 suites. Restaurant, lobby lounge, snack bar, no-smoking rooms, pool. AE, DC, MC, V.

$$–$$$ 🏨 **Ambassador Hotel.** The Ambassador's west-Waikīkī location puts guests in a good position. It's within walking distance of the beach and all that Waikīkī has to offer while close to the new convention center, the Ala Wai Canal, and Ala Moana Shopping Center. There's nothing glamorous about the exterior of this high-rise hotel; the rooms' carpeting, curtains, fixtures, lighting, and furnishings look fresh. All rooms have private lānai, and superior units come with a stove and oven. Keo's Thai restaurant opened here in 1998. ⊠ 2040 Kūhiō Ave., Honolulu, 96815, ☎ 808/941–7777 or 800/923–2620, ℻ 808/941–4717. 187 rooms, 34 suites. Restaurant, in-room safes, kitchenettes, refrigerators, 1 pool. AE, D, DC, MC, V.

$$–$$$ 🏨 **Coconut Plaza Hotel.** With its intimate size and service, Coconut Plaza is a true boutique hotel. On the Ala Wai Canal, three blocks from the beach, its tropical plantation decor features rattan furnishings and floral bedspreads. Guest rooms have private lānai, and all except standard view rooms come with kitchenettes. Free Continental breakfast is served daily on the lobby veranda. ⊠ 450 Lewers St., Honolulu, 96815, ☎ 808/923–8828 or 800/882–9696, ℻ 808/923–3473. 70 rooms, 11 suites. Kitchenettes, pool, meeting rooms. AE, D, DC, MC, V.

$$ 🏨 **Continental Surf Hotel.** One of the better budget hotels of Waikīkī, this appealing high-rise is along the Kūhiō Avenue strip, two blocks from the ocean and convenient to many shops and restaurants. The lobby is large and breezy, and the comfortable rooms are decorated in Polynesian hues of browns and golds. The units have limited views and no lānai. Guests may use the facilities of its sister hotel, the Miramar, 1½ blocks away. ⊠ 2426 Kūhiō Ave., Honolulu,

96815, ☎ *808/922–2232,* ⓕⓐⓧ *808/923–9487. 141 rooms. Kitchenettes. No credit cards.*

$$ 🏨 **Outrigger Royal Islander.** This inexpensive link in the Outrigger hotel chain boasts a great location—just a two-minute walk from a very nice section of Waikīkī Beach. The rooms have tapa-print bedspreads, ceramic lamps, and Island-inspired pictures on the walls. Each room also has a private lānai. Choose between studios, one-bedroom apartments, or suites. The staff is helpful in arranging activities, such as golf and scuba packages and sightseeing tours. Guests have access to pools at other Outrigger hotels. ⊠ *2164 Kālia Rd., Honolulu, 96815,* ☎ *808/922–1961 or 800/688–7444,* ⓕⓐⓧ *808/923–4632. 94 rooms, 7 suites. In-room safes, coin laundry. AE, D, DC, MC, V.*

$–$$ 🏨 **Waikīkī Hana.** Smack dab in the middle of Waikīkī and a block away from the beach, this eight-story hotel is convenient for exploring just about every shop, restaurant, and activity in Oʻahu's tourist hub. Accommodations are clean and plain; many have their own lānai. Pay a little extra per day and you can rent a refrigerator. ⊠ *2424 Koa Ave., Honolulu, 96815,* ☎ *808/926–8841 or 800/367–5004,* ⓕⓐⓧ *808/924–3770. 70 rooms, 2 suites. Restaurant, lobby lounge, in-room safes, kitchenettes, coin laundry. AE, DC, MC, V.*

$ 🏨 **Edmunds Hotel Apartments.** On the Ala Wai Canal, four blocks from the ocean, this has been a budget alternative for decades. Long lānai wrap around the building, so each room has its own view of the pretty canal and glorious Manoa Valley beyond—views that look especially lovely at night, when lights are twinkling up the mountain ridges. If you can put up with the constant sounds of traffic on the boulevard, this is a real bargain. ⊠ *2411 Ala Wai Blvd., Honolulu, 96815,* ☎ *808/923–8381 or 808/732–5169. 12 rooms. Kitchenettes. No credit cards.*

$ 🏨 **Malihini Hotel.** There's no pool, it's not on the beach, none of the units has a TV or air-conditioning, and the rooms are spartan. Still, the atmosphere of this low-rise complex is cool and pleasant, and the gardens are well maintained. All rooms are either studios or one-bedrooms, and all have kitchenettes and daily maid service. The low prices and good location make this a popular place, so be sure to book well in advance. ⊠ *217 Saratoga Rd., Honolulu, 96815,* ☎ *808/*

923–9644. 21 rooms, 9 suites. Kitchenettes. No credit cards.

$ ⚏ **Royal Grove Hotel.** You won't go wrong with this flamingo-pink family-oriented hotel, reminiscent of Miami. With just six floors, it is one of Waikīkī's smaller hotels. The lobby is comfortable; the rooms, though agreeably furnished, have no theme and no views. The pool area is bright with tropical flowers (the hotel is not on the beach). ⊠ *15 Uluniu Ave., Honolulu, 96815,* ☎ *808/923–7691,* ℻ *808/922–7508. 78 rooms, 7 suites. Kitchenettes, pool. AE, D, DC, MC, V.*

Honolulu

$$$$ ⚏ **'Ihilani Resort & Spa.** On O'ahu's western shore, 'Ihi-
★ lani is a 25-minute drive from Honolulu International Airport. Providing a Neighbor Island atmosphere, the resort has a sleek 15-story hotel illuminated by a glass-dome atrium. Guest rooms have marble bathrooms with deep soaking tubs, private lānai with teak furnishings, CD players and a selection of CDs, and a high-tech control system (lights, temperature controls, and more) built into the telephones. Most rooms have ocean views. The 35,000-sq-ft 'Ihilani Spa offers everything from seaweed baths to stair-climbers, and there's a championship golf course and a wonderful brunch. ⊠ *92–1001 'Ōlani St., Kapolei, 96707,* ☎ *808/679–0079 or 800/626–4446,* ℻ *808/679–0295. 333 rooms, 54 suites. 4 restaurants, 2 pools, spa, 18-hole golf course, 6 tennis courts, baby-sitting. AE, DC, MC, V.*

$$$$ ⚏ **Kāhala Mandarin Oriental Hawai'i.** Minutes away from
★ Waikīkī, on the quiet side of Diamond Head, this elegant oceanfront hotel is hidden in the wealthy neighborhood of Kāhala. The room decor combines touches of Asia and old Hawai'i, with mahogany furniture, teak parquet floors, hand-loomed area rugs, local art, and grass-cloth wall coverings. The popular dolphin pool has been expanded; it's now easier to see these friendly creatures. ⊠ *5000 Kāhala Ave., 96816,* ☎ *808/734–2211 or 800/367–2525,* ℻ *808/ 737–2478. 341 rooms, 29 suites. 3 restaurants, 2 lobby lounges, pool, outdoor hot tub, sauna, steam room, exercise room, beach, dive shop, snorkeling, business services, meeting rooms. AE, D, DC, MC, V.*

$$$ 🏨 **Aston Executive Centre Hotel.** Here's a great option for the corporate traveler who wants to avoid Waikīkī. Downtown Honolulu's only hotel is an all-suite high-rise in the center of the business district and 10 minutes from Honolulu International Airport. Suites are on the top 10 floors of a 40-story glass-walled tower, providing views of downtown and Honolulu Harbor. Each unit has a separate living area and kitchenette stocked with cold beverages. ⊠ *1088 Bishop St., 96813,* ☎ *808/539–3000 or 800/949–3932,* FAX *808/523–1088. 116 suites. Restaurant, in-room safes, kitchenettes, pool, exercise room, business services, meeting rooms. CP. AE, DC, MC, V.*

$$–$$$ 🏨 **Ala Moana Hotel.** This longstanding landmark has an excellent location, right next to the popular Ala Moana Shopping Center (they're connected by a pedestrian ramp) and one block from Ala Moana Beach Park. Each room in this 36-story high-rise has a lānai with a view of either the ocean, the Koʻolau Mountains, or Diamond Head. Amenities are modern; you can order room service at the touch of a remote control button. Concierge floor rooms on the 29th to 35th floors offer in-room whirlpool baths and free use of the conference room. ⊠ *410 Atkinson Dr., 96814,* ☎ *808/955–4811 or 800/367–6025,* FAX *808/944–2974. 1,102 rooms, 67 suites. 4 restaurants, bar, 2 lobby lounges, in-room safes, pool, dance club, nightclub, meeting room. AE, DC, MC, V.*

$$–$$$ 🏨 **Mānoa Valley Inn.** Here's an intimate surprise tucked away in Mānoa Valley, just 2 mi from Waikīkī. Built in 1919, this stately hotel serves a complimentary Continental breakfast buffet on a shady lānai and fresh fruit and cheese in the afternoon. Rooms are country-inn style, with antique four-poster beds, marble-top dressers, patterned wallpaper, and fresh flowers; the reading room has a TV and VCR. ⊠ *2001 Vancouver Dr., Honolulu, 96822,* ☎ *808/947–6019 or 800/535–0085,* FAX *800/633–5085. 8 rooms, 4 with private bath; 1 cottage. CP. AE, DC, MC, V.*

$$–$$$ 🏨 **Pagoda Hotel.** The Pagoda's location, along with moderate rates, make this a good choice if you're simply looking for a place to sleep and to catch a couple of meals. It's minutes from Ala Moana Shopping Center and Ala Moana Beach Park, and a free shuttle bus makes the trip between the hotel and its sister property, the Pacific Beach in Waikīkī.

Studio rooms include a full-size refrigerator, a stove, and cooking utensils. There are no great views, since the hotel is surrounded by high-rises. The Pagoda floating restaurant is notable for its Japanese gardens and carp-filled waterways. ⊠ *1525 Rycroft St., Honolulu, 96814,* ☎ *808/941– 6611 or 800/472–4632,* ⅋ᴀ⅋ *808/955–5067. 364 rooms. 2 restaurants, refrigerators, pool. AE, D, DC, MC, V.*

5 Nightlife and the Arts

Updated
by Marty
Wentzel

NIGHTLIFE ON O'AHU can be as simple as a barefoot stroll in the sand or as elaborate as a dinner show with all the glitter of a Las Vegas production. You can view the vibrant hues of a Honolulu sunset during a cocktail cruise, or hear the melodies of ancient chants at a lū'au on a remote beach.

Waikīkī is where nearly all O'ahu's night action takes place—Kalākaua and Kūhiō avenues come to life when the sun goes down and the lights go on. Outside Honolulu, offerings are slimmer but equally diverse. You can dance the two-step at a waterfront café one night and then boogie to live bands in a tiny second-story windward bar the next.

Meanwhile, hula dancers wear sequin skirts in Waikīkī and authentic ti-leaf skirts at Paradise Cove; they are accompanied by everything from *ipu* drums to electric guitars, mercifully not on the same stage in most cases. The latest high-tech, multimedia video discos may also be found, but then, so are acoustic 'ukulele trios.

The arts thrive right alongside the tourist industry in O'ahu's balmy climate. The island has an established symphony, a thriving opera company, chamber music groups, and community theaters. Major Broadway shows, dance companies, and rock stars also make their way to Honolulu. Check the local newspapers—the morning *Honolulu Advertiser* or the afternoon *Honolulu Star-Bulletin*—for the latest happenings.

Bars, Cabarets, and Clubs

Many bars will admit people younger than 21 but will not serve them alcohol. By law, all establishments that serve alcoholic beverages must close at 2 AM. The only exceptions are those with a cabaret license, which have a 4 AM curfew. Though billed as discotheques, they are required to have live music. Most places have a cover charge of $2–$5.

Waikīkī

Banyan Veranda has such Hawaiian entertainers as Jerry Santos and Pumehana Davis, who perform on the open-air lānai. ⊠ *Sheraton Moana Surfrider, 2365 Kalākaua Ave.,* ☎ *808/922–3111.* ☺ *Daily breakfast–11 PM.*

Blue Zebra Café is a mirrored, split-level disco that plays live and recorded music. ⊠ *Restaurant Row, 500 Ala Moana Blvd.,* ☎ *808/538–0409.* ☺ *Nightly 8–4.*

Club 1739. Punk and funk find their home at this dance club, where live bands take turns with DJs keeping twentysomethings up all night. Honolulu's weekly alternative newspaper voted this the best place to dance in Waikīkī. ⊠ *1739 Kalākaua Ave.,* ☎ *808/949–1739.* ☺ *Sun.–Thurs. 9–2, Fri.–Sat. 9 PM–8 AM, live music Thurs. and Sat. 9–midnight.*

Coconuts Nightclub. Blues, jazz, and soul are alive and well at this small nightclub by the Ala Wai Yacht Harbor. ⊠ *'Ilikai Hotel Nikko Waikīkī, 1777 Ala Moana Blvd.,* ☎ *808/949–3811.* ☺ *Live music nightly 8–midnight.*

Cupid's Lobby Bar. A variety of musicians take to the stage in this hotel lounge. Mellow Friday night gigs by local pianist/singer/composer Jay Larrin appeal to a mature crowd. ⊠ *Prince Kūhiō Hotel, 2500 Kūhiō Ave.,* ☎ *808/922–0811.* ☺ *Daily 11–11, live music Tues.–Sat. 7–11.*

Duke's Canoe Club. It's smack dab on Waikīkī Beach, in an old-Hawai'i open-air atmosphere of bamboo, tiki torches, palm-thatch roofs, and luscious koa wood. What better setting in which to sip a mai tai, watch the sunset, and hear some of Hawai'i's most popular musicians? ⊠ *Outrigger Waikīkī Hotel, 2335 Kalākaua Ave.,* ☎ *808/922–2268.* ☺ *Nightly 4–6 and 10–midnight.*

Esprit. Honolulu, an all-male octet, performs music from the big band era of the 1930s up through current pop hits, with Broadway numbers, too. Each band member plays no less than three instruments in this high-energy show. ⊠ *Sheraton Waikīkī Hotel, 2255 Kalākaua Ave.,* ☎ *808/922–4422.* ☺ *Mon.–Tues. 8:30 PM–2 AM.*

Hanohano Room. Late-night jazz prevails during weekly jam sessions by some of Hawai'i's best musicians. They get into everything from jazz to swing to bebop. ⊠ *Sheraton Waikīkī Hotel, 2255 Kalākaua Ave., 30th floor,* ☎ *808/922–4422.* ☺ *Sat. 11 PM–1 AM.*

Lewers Lounge. Singer Loretta Ables performs contemporary jazz and standards here Tuesday through Saturday evenings. A vocalist/pianist sits in Sunday and Monday. A dessert menu is offered. ⊠ *Halekūlani, 2199 Kālia Rd.,* ☎ *808/923–2311.* ⊙ *Nightly 9–12:30.*

Mai Tai Bar. Keith and Carmen Haugen sing island duets at this open-air Waikīkī Beach bar. Carmen's hula is a thing of beauty. Catch them Tuesday and Wednesday; entertainers vary on other nights. ⊠ *Royal Hawaiian Hotel, 2259 Kalākaua Ave.,* ☎ *808/923–7311.* ⊙ *Nightly 5:30–7:30.*

Moose McGillycuddy's Pub and Cafe. Loud bands play for the beach-and-beer gang in a blue-jeans-and-T-shirt setting. ⊠ *310 Lewers St.,* ☎ *808/923–0751.* ⊙ *Nightly 9–1:30.*

Nicholas Nickolas. A splendid view, good music, and a well-dressed crowd somehow come together here as a bit stiff and stuffy. But, hey! Who says you can't make your own fun if the mood and the music click? ⊠ *Ala Moana Hotel, 410 Atkinson Dr.,* ☎ *808/955–4466.* ⊙ *Dancing Sun.–Thurs. 9:30 PM–2 AM, Fri. and Sat. 10 PM–3 AM.*

Nick's Fishmarket. This is probably the most comfortable of Waikīkī's upscale dance lounges, with an elegant crowd, smooth music, and an intimate, dark atmosphere. There's some singles action here. ⊠ *Waikīkī Gateway Hotel, 2070 Kalākaua Ave.,* ☎ *808/955–6333.* ⊙ *Nightly 9–1:30.*

Paradise Lounge. A variety of acts, including the longtime band Olomana, perform in this pretty outdoor club. ⊠ *Hilton Hawaiian Village, 2005 Kālia Rd.,* ☎ *808/949–4321.* ⊙ *Fri. and Sat. 8 PM–midnight.*

Pool Stage. Throughout the week, by the hotel's oceanfront pool, various local performers present outstanding Hawaiian song and dance. One of the most popular mainstays is 'ukulele wizard Moe Keale, familiar to TV viewers from his roles on *Hawai'i Five-O.* ⊠ *Sheraton Waikīkī Hotel, 2255 Kalākaua Ave.,* ☎ *808/922–4422.* ⊙ *Nightly 6–8:30.*

Royal Garden at Waikīkī. Some of O'ahu's top jazz stylists like singing in the elegant, intimate lobby lounge of this sidestreet hotel. ⊠ *Royal Garden at Waikīkī, 444 'Olohana St.,* ☎ *808/943–0202.* ⊙ *Tues.–Sun. 8–11.*

Rumours. The after-work crowd loves this spot, which has dance videos, disco, and throbbing lights. On Big Chill nights each Friday the club plays oldies from the '60s and '70s and serves free pūpū. There's ballroom dancing Sunday evening from 5 to 9. ⊠ *Ala Moana Hotel, 410 Atkinson St.,* ☎ *808/ 955–4811.* ☾ *Wed.–Fri. 5 PM–2 AM, Sat. 8 PM–4 AM.*

Scruples. There's disco dancing to Top 40 tunes, with a young-adult, mostly local crowd. The Thursday night bikini contest packs 'em in. ⊠ *Waikīkī Market Place, 2310 Kūhiō Ave.,* ☎ *808/923–9530.* ☾ *Nightly 8–4.*

Shore Bird Beach Broiler. This beachfront disco spills right out onto the sand; it features a large dance floor and 10-ft video screen. Karaoke sing-alongs are held nightly. ⊠ *Outrigger Reef Hotel, 2169 Kālia Rd.,* ☎ *808/922–2887.* ☾ *Nightly 9–2.*

Wave Waikīkī. Dance to live rock and roll until 1:30 AM, recorded music after that. It can be a rough scene, but the bands are tops. ⊠ *1877 Kalākaua Ave.,* ☎ *808/941–0424.* ☾ *Nightly 9–4.*

Honolulu

Anna Bannana's. At this two-story, smoky dive, the live music is fresh, loud, and sometimes experimental. Different local favorites deliver ultracreative dancing music, and the likes of blues singer Taj Mahal have been known to slip in for a set or two. ⊠ *2440 S. Beretania St.,* ☎ *808/946– 5190.* ☾ *Nightly 11:30–2, live music Thurs.–Sat. 9–2.*

Gordon Biersch Brewery Restaurant. Live duos and trios serenade patrons of the outside bar that flanks Honolulu Harbor. While there's no dancing, this is the place in Honolulu to see and be seen. ⊠ *Aloha Tower Marketplace, 101 Ala Moana Blvd.,* ☎ *808/599–4877.* ☾ *Wed.–Sat. 7 PM–1 AM.*

Pier Bar. Here's one of the few places in Honolulu to hear live music outdoors. The Pier Bar attracts a grab bag of groups; call ahead to find out who's playing. ⊠ *Aloha Tower Marketplace, 101 Ala Moana Blvd.,* ☎ *808/536– 2166.* ☾ *Nightly 6:30–4.*

Row Bar. Restaurant Row's outdoor gathering place mixes it up each weekend with live reggae, rock, and rhythm 'n' blues. Single professionals meet here *pau hana* (after work).

⊠ *Restaurant Row, 500 Ala Moana Blvd.,* ☎ *808/528–2345.* ☉ *Fri.–Sat. 8–11:45, Sun. jazz 5:30–8:30.*

Sand Island Rhythm & Blues. When red-hot blues acts from the mainland come to town, they often play in this small bar near downtown Honolulu. A high-tech sound system does them justice. Opening hours vary; check local papers or call ahead. ⊠ *197 Sand Island Access Rd.,* ☎ *808/847–4274.*

World Cafe. Honolulu's only upscale billiards nightclub also has a sports bar and dancing to Top 40 tunes. ⊠ *Restaurant Row, 500 Ala Moana Blvd.,* ☎ *808/599–4450.* ☉ *Mon.–Thurs. 11:30 AM–2 AM, Fri. and Sat. 11:30 AM–4 AM, Sun. 3 PM–2 AM.*

Kailua

Fast Eddie's. If you want to boogie, visit this hot spot for local and national bands playing everything from rock to Top 40. Attention, ladies: The Fast Eddie's Male Revue is a longstanding tradition not to be missed. ⊠ *52 Oneawa St.,* ☎ *808/261–8561.*

Cocktail and Dinner Cruises

Most of the following boats set sail daily from Fisherman's Wharf at Kewalo Basin, just 'ewa of Ala Moana Beach Park, and head along the coast toward Diamond Head. There's usually dinner, dancing, drinks, and a sensational sunset. Except as noted, dinner cruises cost approximately $50–$60, cocktail cruises $20–$30.

Ali'i Kai Catamaran. Patterned after an ancient Polynesian vessel, this huge catamaran casts off from historic Aloha Tower with 1,000 passengers. The deluxe dinner cruise has two open bars, a huge dinner, and an authentic Polynesian show with colorful hula music. The food is good, the after-dinner show loud and fun, and everyone dances on the way back to shore. ⊠ *Pier 5, street level, Honolulu,* ☎ *808/539–9400.* ☉ *Nightly at 5:30.*

Dream Cruises. The 100-ft motor yacht *American Dream* handles up to 225 guests for evening cruises off the shores of Waikīkī. Decks have plenty of outdoor space for views of the city lights. The dinner cruise includes one mai tai, buffet, and soft drinks; you pay for extra booze. After a

BONUS MILES MAKE GREAT SOUVENIRS.

Earn Miles With Your MCI Card.

Take the MCI Card along on this trip and start earning miles for the next one. You'll earn frequent flyer miles on all your calls and save with the low rates you've come to expect from MCI. Before you know it, you'll be on your way to some other international destination.

Sign up for MCI by calling 1-800-FLY-FREE

*U.S. dollar equivalent, net of taxes, credits and discounts. All airline program rules and conditions apply. Other terms and conditions apply to ongoing mileage offer and bonus mile offer. MCI, its logo and the names of the products and services referred to herein are proprietary marks of MCI Communications Corporation. American Airlines reserves the right to change the AAdvantage program at any time without notice. American Airlines is not responsible for products and services offered by other participating companies. American Airlines and AAdvantage are registered trademarks of American Airlines, Inc.

Is this a great time, or what? :-)

Earn Frequent Flyer Miles.

AmericanAirlines
AAdvantage

Continental Airlines
OnePass

Delta Air Lines
SkyMiles

HAWAIIAN
AIRLINES.

MIDWEST EXPRESS
AIRLINES

NORTHWEST
AIRLINES
WORLDPERKS

Rapid Rewards
SOUTHWEST AIRLINES

MILEAGE PLUS.
United Airlines

US AIRWAYS
DIVIDEND MILES

With guidebooks for every kind of travel—from weekend getaways to island hopping to adventures abroad—it's easy to understand why smart travelers go with **Fodor's**.

At bookstores everywhere.
www.fodors.com

Smart travelers go with **Fodor's**™

hula demonstration with audience participation, a disc jockey spins tunes from the '50s through the '70s. ⊠ *1085 Ala Moana Blvd., Suite 103, Honolulu,* ☎ *808/592–5200.*

Paradise Cruises. Prices vary depending on which deck you choose on the 1,600-passenger, four-deck *Star of Honolulu.* For instance, a seven-course French dinner on the top costs $199, while a steak and crab feast on level two costs $72. Evening excursions also take place on the 340-passenger *Starlet I* and 230-passenger *Starlet II.* ⊠ *1540 S. King St., Honolulu,* ☎ *808/593–2493.*

Royal Hawaiian Cruises. The sleek *Navatek* is a revolutionary craft designed to sail smoothly in rough waters. That allows it to power farther along Waikīkī's coastline than its competitors. During the cocktail cruise, there's sizzling entertainment by such local singers as Nohelani Cypriano, and the dinner cruise includes gourmet food by acclaimed Maui chef George Mavrothalassitis. ⊠ *Honolulu Harbor,* ☎ *808/848–6360.* ☉ *Dinner cruise nightly 5:30–8.*

Tradewind Charters. This is a real sailing experience, a little more expensive and a lot more intimate than the other cruises mentioned. The three-hour sunset sail carries no more than six people. Champagne and hors d'oeuvres are extra. ⊠ *1833 Kalākaua Ave., Suite 612, Honolulu,* ☎ *808/ 973–0311.*

Windjammer Cruises. The pride of the fleet is the 1,000-passenger *Kulamanu,* done up like a clipper ship. Formerly the *Rella Mae,* it was once a Hudson River excursion boat in New York. Cocktails, dinner, a Polynesian revue, and dancing to a live band are all part of the package. Prices vary from $49 for a dinner buffet to $100 for the deluxe steak and lobster spread. ⊠ *Pier 7, Honolulu Harbor, Honolulu,* ☎ *808/537–1122.* ☉ *Nightly at sunset.*

Cocktail and Dinner Shows

Some O'ahu entertainers have been around for years, and others have just arrived on the scene. The dinner-show food is usually acceptable, but certainly not the main reason for coming. Dinner shows are all in the $45–$60 range; cocktail shows run $30–$35. The prices usually include one cocktail, tax, and gratuity. In all cases, reservations are essential, and most major credit cards are accepted. Be sure to call in advance; you never know when an artist may have switched venues.

Charo. The "coochie-coochie" girl's latest show takes place in one of Waikīkī's most popular showrooms, one block from the beach. Latin rhythms, flamenco dancing, songs of the Islands, and international music add up to a fiery evening with this explosive performer. ⊠ *Polynesian Palace, Outrigger Reef Towers Hotel, 227 Lewers St.,* ☎ *808/ 923–7469.* ☉ *Tues.–Sat. at 7.*

Don Ho. Waikīkī's old pro still packs them in for his Polynesian revue (with a cast of young and attractive Hawaiian performers), which has found the perfect home in an intimate club. ⊠ *Waikīkī Beachcomber Hotel, 2300 Kalākaua Ave.,* ☎ *808/931–3009.* ☉ *Candlelight dinner show Tues.–Fri. and Sun. at 7, cocktail show Tues.–Fri. and Sun. at 9.*

Frank DeLima. Local funny man Frank DeLima places a heavy accent on the ethnic humor of the Islands and does some pretty outrageous impressions. By the end of the evening he's poked fun at everyone in the audience—and folks eat it up. A word of caution: Reserve a stageside table only if you're up for a personal ribbing. ⊠ *Hula Hut, 286 Beach Walk,* ☎ *808/923–8411.* ☉ *Fri.–Sat. at 8:45.*

Kalo's Polynesian South Seas Revue. This musical excursion features songs and dances from Tahiti, Tonga, and the Hawaiian Islands. Two shows nightly include an all-you-can-eat prime-rib buffet. ⊠ *Hawaiian Hut Theater Restaurant, Ala Moana Hotel, 410 Atkinson Dr.,* ☎ *808/941–5205.* ☉ *Dinner seating nightly at 5:30, show nightly at 6:30.*

Legends in Concert. Elvis Presley, Madonna, and Michael Jackson look- and sound-alikes take to the stage at this glitzy extravaganza. The setting is an elaborate 1,000-seat showroom with a million-dollar sound and light system. Featuring backup singers and dancers and special effects, it's patterned after a Las Vegas show of the same name. ⊠ *Aloha Showroom, Royal Hawaiian Shopping Center,* ☎ *808/971– 1400.* ☉ *Nightly at 6:30 and 9.*

Magic of Polynesia. Magician John Hirokawa displays mystifying sleight-of-hand in this highly entertaining show, which also includes the requisite hula dancers and Island music. ⊠ *Hilton Hawaiian Village Dome, 2005 Kālia Rd.,* ☎ *808/949–4321.* ☉ *Nightly at 6:30 and 8:45.*

Sheraton's Spectacular Polynesian Revue. From drumbeats of the ancient Hawaiians to Fijian war dances and Samoan slap dances, this show takes audiences on a musical tour of Polynesia. The highlight is a daring Samoan fire knife dancer. A fashion show precedes the evening entertainment. ⊠ *'Ainahau Showroom, Sheraton Princess Ka'iulani Hotel, 120 Ka'iulani Ave.,* ☎ *808/922–5811.* ☉ *Dinner seatings nightly at 5:15 and 8, cocktail seatings nightly at 5:45 and 8:15, shows nightly at 6 and 8:30.*

Society of Seven. This lively, popular septet has great staying power and, after more than 25 years, continues to put on one of the best shows in Waikīkī. They sing, dance, do impersonations, play instruments, and above all, entertain with their contemporary sound. ⊠ *Outrigger Waikīkī Hotel, 2335 Kalākaua Ave.,* ☎ *808/923–0711.* ☉ *Mon.– Sat. at 9; extra show Wed., Fri., and Sat. at 7.*

Dance

Every year, at least one of mainland America's finer ballet troupes makes the trip to Honolulu for a series of dance performances at the **Neal Blaisdell Center Concert Hall** (⊠ Ward Ave. at King St., Honolulu, ☎ 808/591–2211). A local company, **Ballet Hawai'i** (☎ 808/988–7578), is active during the holiday season with its annual production of *The Nutcracker,* which is usually held at the Mamiya Theater (⊠ 3142 Wai'alae Ave., Chaminade University, Honolulu).

Film

Art, international, classic, and silent films are screened at the little theater at the **Honolulu Academy of Arts.** ⊠ 900 S. Beretania St., Honolulu, ☎ 808/532–8768. ☝ $4.

The **Hawai'i International Film Festival** (⊠ 700 Bishop St., Suite 400, Honolulu, ☎ 808/528–3456) may not be Cannes, but it is unique and exciting. During the weeklong festival, held from the end of November to early December, top films from the United States, Asia, and the Pacific are screened day and night at several theaters on O'ahu.

Varsity Theater (✉ 1106 University Ave., Honolulu, ☎ 808/973–5834) is a two-theater art house that brings internationally acclaimed motion pictures to Honolulu.

Waikīkī generally gets the first-run films at its trio of theaters dubbed, appropriately, the **Waikīkī 1, Waikīkī 2, and Waikīkī 3** (☎ 808/971–5033). Check newspapers for what's playing.

Kāhala Mall (✉ 4211 Wai'alae Ave., Honolulu, ☎ 808/733–6233) has eight movie theaters showing a diverse range of films. It's a 10-minute drive from Waikīkī.

Lū'au

Here are some good lū'au that emphasize fun over strict adherence to tradition. They generally cost $40–$75. Reservations are essential.

Germaine's Lū'au. You and a herd of about 1,000 other people are bused to a private beach near the industrial area, 35 minutes from Waikīkī. The bus ride is actually a lot of fun, and the beach and the sunset are pleasant. The service is brisk in order to feed everyone on time, and the food is so-so, but the show is warm and friendly. The bus collects passengers from 13 Waikīkī hotels. ☎ *808/941–3338.* ☉ *Lū'au start at 6 Tues.–Sun.*

Paradise Cove Lū'au. This is another mass-produced event for 1,000 or so. Once again, a bus takes you from one of six Waikīkī hotel pickup points to a remote beach beside a picturesque cove on the western side of the island, 27 mi from Waikīkī. There are palms and a glorious sunset, and the pageantry is fun, even informative. The food—well, you didn't come for the food, did you? ☎ *808/973–5828.* ☉ *Lū'au begin daily at 5:30, doors open at 5.*

Polynesian Cultural Center Lū'au. An hour's drive from Honolulu, this North Shore O'ahu attraction takes place amid seven re-created villages of Polynesia. Dinner is all-you-can-eat, followed by a world-class revue. ☎ *808/923–1861.* ☺ *Mon.–Sat. at 5:30.*

Royal Hawaiian Lūʻau. This is a notch above the rest of the commercial lūʻau on Oʻahu, perhaps because it takes place at the wonderful Pink Palace. With the setting sun, Diamond Head, the Pacific Ocean, and the enjoyable entertainment, who cares if the lūʻau isn't totally authentic? ☎ *808/923–7311.* ☺ *Mon. at 6.*

Music

Chamber Music Hawaiʻi (☎ 808/947–1975) gives 25 concerts a year at the Honolulu Lutheran Church (✉ 1730 Punahou St., Honolulu), Honolulu Academy of Arts (✉ 900 S. Beretania St., Honolulu), and other locations.

Hawaiʻi Opera Theater's season spans January through March, and includes such works as *Romeo and Juliet, Don Giovanni,* and *Macbeth.* All are performed in their original language with projected English translation. ✉ *Neal Blaisdell Concert Hall, Ward Ave. and King St., Honolulu,* ☎ *808/596–7858.* 🎟 *$20–$65 at box office.*

Honolulu Symphony Orchestra, led by a young and dynamic conductor named Samuel Wong, is a top-notch ensemble whether it's playing by itself or backing up a guest artist. International performers are headlined from time to time, and pops programs are also offered. Write or call for a complete schedule. Shows take place at the Blaisdell Center and Hawaiʻi Theatre Center. ✉ *677 Ala Moana Blvd., Honolulu,* ☎ *808/524–0815.* 🎟 *$10–$50.*

During the school year, the faculty of the **University of Hawaiʻi Music Department** (☎ 808/956–8742) gives concerts at Orvis Auditorium on the Manoa campus.

Rock concerts are usually performed at the cavernous **Neal Blaisdell Center Arena** (☎ 808/591–2211).

Internationally famous performers pack them in at **Aloha Stadium** (☎ 808/486–9300). Check newspapers for upcoming events.

Theater

Because the Islands are so expensive to get to and stay on, major touring companies seldom come to Hawai'i. As a result, O'ahu has developed several excellent local theater troupes, which present first-rate entertainment on an amateur and semiprofessional level all year long.

Army Community Theatre is a favorite for its revivals of musical theater classics, presented in an 800-seat house. The casts are talented and the fare is great for families. ⊠ *Richardson Theater, Fort Shafter, Honolulu,* ☎ *808/438–4480.* 🎭 *$12–$15.*

Diamond Head Theater is in residence five minutes away from Waikīkī, right next to Diamond Head. Its repertoire includes a little of everything: musicals, dramas, experimental, contemporary, and classics. ⊠ *520 Makapu'u Ave., Honolulu,* ☎ *808/734–0274.* 🎭 *$10–$40.*

The beautiful **Hawai'i Theatre Center** in downtown Honolulu, built in the 1920s, hosts a wide range of events, including theatrical productions. ⊠ *1130 Bethel St., Honolulu,* ☎ *808/528–0506.* 🎭 *Prices vary.*

🐚 **Honolulu Theater for Youth** stages delightful productions for children around the Islands from July to May. Write or call for a schedule. ⊠ *2846 Ualena St., Honolulu,* ☎ *808/ 839–9885.* 🎭 *$10.*

John F. Kennedy Theater at the University of Hawai'i's Manoa campus is the setting for eclectic dramatic offerings—everything from musical theater to Kabuki, Noh, and Chinese opera. ⊠ *1770 East–West Rd., Honolulu,* ☎ *808/ 956–7655.* 🎭 *$7–$12.*

Kumu Kahua is the only troupe presenting shows and plays written on and about the Islands. It stages five or six productions a year. ⊠ *46 Merchant St., Honolulu,* ☎ *808/536–4441.* 🎭 *$12–$15.*

Manoa Valley Theater gives wonderful nonprofessional performances in an intimate theater in Manoa Valley from September to July. ⊠ *2833 E. Manoa Rd., Honolulu,* ☎ *808/988–6131.* 🎭 *$23–$25.*

6 Outdoor Activities, Sports, and Beaches

Participant Sports

Biking

The good news is that the coastal roads are flat and well paved. On the downside, they're also awash in vehicular traffic. Frankly, biking is no fun in either Waikīkī or Honolulu, but things are a bit better outside the city. Be sure to take along a nylon jacket for the frequent showers on the windward side and remember that Hawai'i is Paradise after the Fall: Lock up your bike.

Mountain bikes are available for rent at **Blue Sky Rentals & Sports Center** (⊠ 1920 Ala Moana Blvd., across from the Hilton Hawaiian Village, ☎ 808/947–0101). Rates are $15 a day (8–6) or $20 for 24 hours plus a $25 deposit; this includes a bike, a helmet, a lock, and a water bottle.

You buy a bike or, if you brought your own, you can get it repaired at **Eki Cyclery Shop** (⊠ 1603 Dillingham Blvd., Honolulu, ☎ 808/847–2005). If you want to find some biking buddies, write ahead to the **Hawai'i Bicycling League** (⊠ Box 4403, Honolulu 96813, ☎ 808/735–5756), which can tell you about upcoming races (frequent on all the Islands).

Fitness Centers

Clark Hatch Physical Fitness Center has weight-training facilities, an indoor pool, a racquetball court, aerobics classes, treadmills, and indoor-running apparatus. ⊠ 745 Fort St., Honolulu, ☎ 808/536–7205. 🖃 About $10 per day. ☉ Weekdays 6 AM–8 PM, Sat. 7:30–5:30.

'Ihilani Resort & Spa (⊠ Ko Olina Resort, Kapolei, ☎ 808/679–0079), about 30 minutes from the airport, has O'ahu's largest health and fitness center, with 35,000 square ft of space for classes, weight rooms, relaxation programs, hydrotherapies—you name it. Call to arrange nonguest privileges.

24-Hour Fitness is Waikīkī's most accessible fitness center. There are weight-training machines, cardiovascular equipment, free weights, and a pro shop. ⊠ Pacific Beach Hotel, 2nd floor, 2490 Kalākaua Ave., ☎ 808/971–4653. 🖃 $10 per day for guests of many Waikīkī hotels (call for list), $20 nonguests. ☉ Daily.

Golf

O'ahu has more golf courses than any other Hawaiian island. One of the most popular facilities is the **Ala Wai Golf Course** on Waikīkī's mauka end, across the Ala Wai Canal. It's par 70 on 6,424 yards and has a pro shop and a restaurant. The waiting list is long, so if you plan to play, call the minute you land. ☒ *404 Kapahulu Ave.,* ☎ *808/733–7387.* ☒ *Greens fee: $40; cart $14.*

Advance reservations are recommended at the 18-hole, 6,222-yard **Hawai'i Kai Championship Course** and the neighboring 18-hole, 2,386-yard **Hawai'i Kai Executive Course.** ☒ *8902 Kalaniana'ole Hwy., Honolulu,* ☎ *808/395–2358.* ☒ *Greens fee: weekdays $85 and $37, respectively; weekends and holidays $95 and $42. Cart included.*

Ko Olina Golf Club is affiliated with the Ihilani Resort on Oahu's west side. Its 18 holes are beautifully landscaped with waterfalls and ponds where black and white swans serve as your gallery. ☒ *Ko Olina Resort, 92-1220 Ali'inui Dr., Kapolei,* ☎ *808/676–5300.* ☒ *Greens fee: $95 guests, $145 nonguests.*

Horseback Riding

Kualoa Ranch (☒ 49-560 Kamehameha Hwy., Ka'a'awa, ☎ 808/237–8515 or 808/538–7636 in Honolulu), on the windward side, across from Kualoa Beach Park, leads trail rides in Ka'a'awa, one of the most beautiful valleys in all Hawai'i. Kualoa has other activities as well, like windsurfing and jet skiing. Try one of their all-inclusive packages, starting at $79, with transportation from Waikīkī and a choice of activities.

Jogging

In Honolulu, the most popular places are the two parks, **Kapi'olani** and **Ala Moana,** at either end of Waikīkī. In both cases, the loop around the park is just under 2 mi. You can run a 4½-mi ring around **Diamond Head crater,** past scenic views, luxurious homes, and herds of other joggers.

If you jog along the 1½-mi **Ala Wai Canal,** you'll probably glimpse outrigger-canoe teams practicing on the canal. If you're looking for jogging companions, show up for the free **Honolulu Marathon Clinic** that starts at the Kapi'olani Park Bandstand, March–November, Sunday 7:30 AM.

Once you leave Honolulu, it gets trickier to find places to jog that are scenic as well as safe. Best to stick to the well-traveled routes, or ask the experienced folks at the **Running Room** (⊠ 819 Kapahulu Ave., Honolulu, ☎ 808/737–2422) for advice.

Rock Climbing

The Mokulēʻia Wall on the North Shore is one of the world's best venues for rock climbing. This 900-ft vertical trail is as challenging as any in the world. Those skilled enough to make it to the top get glorious views of the coastline. From Farrington Highway (Hwy. 930), west of Haleiwa, there is a trail leading to the base of the Mokulēʻia Wall, but the trailhead is poorly marked and easy to miss. For help in finding it, call or visit the experts at **Climbers Paradise** (⊠ 214 Sand Island Rd., Honolulu ☎ 808/842–7625), an indoor climbing center that also rents gear and offers lessons.

Tennis

In the Waikīkī area, there are four free public courts at **Kapiʻolani Tennis Courts** (⊠ 2748 Kalākaua Ave., ☎ 808/971–2525); nine at the **Diamond Head Tennis Center** (⊠ 3908 Pākī Ave., ☎ 808/971–7150); and 10 at **Ala Moana Park** (⊠ Makai side of Ala Moana Blvd., ☎ 808/522–7031).

Several Waikīkī hotels have tennis facilities open to nonguests, but guests have first priority. The **ʻIlikai Hotel Nikko Waikīkī** (⊠ 1777 Ala Moana Blvd., ☎ 808/949–3811) has seven courts, one lighted for night play, plus a pro shop, tennis clinics, and a ball machine. The hotel also offers special tennis packages. There's one championship tennis court at the **Hawaiian Regent Hotel** (⊠ 2552 Kalākaua Ave., ☎ 808/922–6611). There are two courts at the **Pacific Beach Hotel** (⊠ 2490 Kalākaua Ave., ☎ 808/922–1233); instruction is available.

Water Sports

The seemingly endless ocean options can be arranged through any hotel travel desk or beach concession. Try the **Waikīkī Beach Center,** next to the Sheraton Moana Surfrider, or the **C & K Beach Service** by the Hilton Hawaiian Village (no telephones).

DEEP-SEA FISHING

For fun on the high seas try **Coreene-C Sport Fishing Charters** (☎ 808/226–8421), **Island Charters** (☎ 808/593–9455), **Tradewind Charters** (☎ 808/973–0311), or **ELO-1 Sport Fishing** (☎ 808/947–5208). All are berthed in Honolulu's Kewalo Basin. Plan to spend from $100 to $115 per person to share a boat for a full day (6:30–3). Half-day (five-hour) rates are $90. Boat charters start at about $550 for a full day and $450 for a half day. Some companies have a six-hour private charter rate of $500. All fishing gear is included, but lunch is not. The captain usually expects to keep the fish. Tipping is customary, and $20 to the captain is not excessive, especially if you keep the fish you caught.

OCEAN KAYAKING

This dynamic sport is catching on fast in the Islands. You sit on top of a board and paddle on both sides; it's great fun for catching waves or just exploring the coastline. Bob Twogood, a name that is synonymous with O'ahu kayaking, runs a shop called **Twogood Kayaks Hawai'i** (✉ 345 Hahani St., Kailua, ☎ 808/262–5656), which makes, rents, and sells the fiberglass craft. Twogood rents solo kayaks for $22 a half day, and $28 for a full day; tandems are $29 a half day and $39 for a full day, including kayak delivery and pickup across from Kailua Beach.

SAILING

Lessons may be arranged through **Tradewind Charters** (✉ 1833 Kalākaua Ave., Honolulu, ☎ 808/973–0311). Instruction follows American Sailing Association standards. The cost for a one-hour private sailing lesson is $65 per person. Transportation from Waikīkī is available. Tradewind specializes in intimate three-hour sunset sails for a maximum of six people at $75 per person, including hors d'oeuvres, champagne, and other beverages. Moonlight sails can be scheduled on an exclusive basis. Ready to take the plunge? Ask about their shipboard weddings.

SCUBA DIVING AND SNORKELING

For scuba diving, **South Seas Aquatics** (✉ 2155 Kalākaua Ave., Suite 112, Honolulu, ☎ 808/922–0852) offers two-tank boat dives for $75. Several certification courses are available; call for rates. **Captain Bruce's Scuba Charters** (☎ 808/373–3590) focuses on trips for experienced divers. Led by a naturalist guide, charters run out of O'ahu's west coast, known for its great scuba sites. A two-tank boat dive costs $104 per person including transportation from Waikīkī, equipment, and refreshments.

The most famous snorkeling spot in Hawai'i is Hanauma Bay. **Hanauma Bay Snorkeling Excursions** (☎ 808/373–5060) runs to and from Waikīkī and costs $21 round-trip, including park admission, snorkeling gear, and lessons. **Hanauma Bay Snorkeling Tours & Rentals** (☎ 808/944–8828) has a half-day Hanauma Bay excursion for the same price.

Area dive sites include: **Maunalua Bay,** east of Diamond Head, has several sites, including Turtle Canyon, with lava flow ridges and sandy canyons teeming with green sea turtles of all sizes; *Kāhala Barge,* a penetrable, 200-ft sunken vessel; Big Eel Reef, with many varieties of moray eels; and Fantasy Reef, a series of lava ledges and archways populated with barracuda and eels.

Mahi Wai'anae is a 165-ft minesweeper sunk in 1982 to create an artificial reef. It's intact and penetrable. Goatfish, tame lemon butterfly fish, blue-striped snapper, and a 6-ft moray eel can be seen hanging about. Depths are from 50 ft to 90 ft.

Hanauma Bay, east of Koko Head, is an underwater state park and a popular dive site. The shallow inner reef gradually drops from 10 ft to 70 ft at the outer reef. Among the tame, colorful tropical fish you'll see here are butterfly fish, goatfish, parrot fish, and surgeon fish; there are also sea turtles.

SURFING

To rent a board in Waikīkī, contact **C & K Beach Service,** on the beach fronting the Hilton Hawaiian Village (☎ no phone). Rentals cost $8–$10 per hour, depending on the size of the board, and $12 for two hours. Lessons are $30 per hour with board, and they promise to have you riding the waves by lesson's end.

WATERSKIING

Suyderhoud Water Ski Center (✉ Koko Marina Shopping Center, 7192 Kalaniana'ole Hwy., Hawai'i Kai, ☎ 808/395–

3773) has a package with round-trip transportation from Waikīkī and a half day of waterskiing in Hawai'i Kai Marina for $99 per person. A 30-minute lesson costs $490; four-passenger ski boat rental is $98 per hour.

WINDSURFING

This sport was born in Hawai'i, and O'ahu's Kailua Beach is its cradle. World champion Robby Naish and his family build and sell boards, rent equipment, run "windsurfari" tours, and offer instruction out of **Naish Hawai'i** (✉ 155A Hāmākua Dr., Kailua, ☎ 808/261–6067). A four-hour package, including 90 minutes of instruction, costs $55.

Windsurfing Hawai'i (✉ 155A Hāmākua Dr., Kailua, ☎ 808/261–3539) carries a complete line of boardsailing equipment and accessories. **Kailua Sailboard Company** (✉ 130 Kailua Rd., Kailua, ☎ 808/262–2555) rents equipment and transports it to the waterfront five minutes away.

Spectator Sports

Football

The nationally-televised **Jeep Aloha Bowl Football Classic,** held on Christmas Day at Aloha Stadium in Honolulu (☎ 808/486–9300), is a sports tradition bringing together powerhouse college teams from the PAC-10 and BIG-12 conferences. For local action the **University of Hawai'i Rainbows** take to the field at Aloha Stadium in season, with a big local following. There are often express buses from Kapi'olani Park (☎ 808/956–6508 for details).

Golf

The giants of the greens return to Hawai'i every January or February (depending on the TV scheduling) to compete in the **Hawaiian Open Golf Tournament** (☎ 808/526–1232), a PGA tour regular with a $1 million purse. It is held at the exclusive Wai'alae Country Club near Waikīkī, and it's always mobbed.

Mountain Biking

Professional mountain bikers come to O'ahu each year for the **Outrigger Hotels Hawaiian Mountain Tour,** a four-day, five-stage race across the most rugged terrain of the windward coast.

Running

The **Honolulu Marathon** is a thrilling event to watch as well as to participate in. Join the throngs who cheer at the finish line at Kapiʻolani Park as internationally famous and local runners tackle the 26.2-mi challenge. It's held on a Sunday in early December and is sponsored by the Honolulu Marathon Association (☎ 808/734–7200).

Triathlon

Swim-bike-run events are gaining in popularity and number in Hawaiʻi. Most fun to watch (or enter) is the **Tinman Triathlon** (☎ 808/732–7311), held in mid-July in Waikīkī.

Volleyball

This is an extremely popular sport in the Islands, and no wonder. Both the men's and women's teams of the **University of Hawaiʻi** have blasted to a number-one league ranking in years past. Crowded, noisy, and very exciting home games are played from September–December (women's) and January–April (men's) in the university's 10,000-seat special-events arena. ⊠ *Lower Campus Rd., Honolulu,* ☎ *808/956–4481.* ▨ *$8.*

Windsurfing

Watch the pros jump and spin on the waves during July's **Pan Am Hawaiian Windsurfing World Cup** off Kailua Beach. There are also windsurfing competitions off Diamond Head point, including August's **Wahine Classic,** featuring the world's best female boardsailors. Consult the sports section of the daily newspaper for details on these events.

Beaches

For South Seas sun, fun, and surf, Hawaiʻi is a dream destination, but first some words of caution: When approaching any Hawaiian beach, take notice of the signs! If they warn of dangerous surf conditions or currents, pay attention. Before you stretch out beneath a swaying palm, check it for coconuts: The trade winds can bring them tumbling down on top of you with enough force to cause serious injury. Don't forget to use sunscreen and reapply it often, especially after swimming. Waikīkī is only 21 degrees north of the equator, and the ultraviolet rays are much more potent than they are at home. No alcoholic beverages are allowed on the beaches here, and no matter which beach you choose, it's best to lock your car.

Waikīkī Beaches

The 2½-mi strand called Waikīkī Beach actually extends from Hilton Hawaiian Village on one end to Kapiʻolani Park and Diamond Head on the other. Areas along this sandy strip have separate names but subtle differences. The Waikīkī Beach Center, opposite the Hyatt Regency Waikīkī, is where you can find rest rooms, showers, a police station, and surfboard lockers. Beach areas are listed here from west to east.

Kahanamoku Beach and Lagoon. The lagoon's calm waters are safe for small children, and you can lazily paddle around it in a little boat. The beach has decent snorkeling and swimming and a gentle surf; its sandy bottom slopes gradually. Named for Hawaiʻi's famous Olympic swimming champion, Duke Kahanamoku, the area has a snack concession, showers, a beach-gear and surfboard rental shop, catamaran cruises, and a sand volleyball court. ⊠ *In front of Hilton Hawaiian Village.*

Ft. DeRussy Beach. Sunbathers, swimmers, and windsurfers enjoy this beach, the widest in Waikīkī. It trails off to a coral ocean bottom with fairly good snorkeling sights. The beach is frequented by military personnel but is open to everyone. There are volleyball courts, food stands, picnic tables, dressing rooms, and showers. ⊠ *In front of Ft. DeRussy and Hale Koa Hotel.*

Gray's Beach. Named for a little lodging house called Gray's-by-the-Sea that stood here in the 1920s, this beach is best known for the two good surfing spots called Paradise and Number Threes just beyond its reef. High tides often cover the narrow beach. The Hawaiians used to consider this a place for spiritual healing and baptism and called it *Kawehewehe* (the removal). You'll find food stands, surfboard and beach-gear rental shops, and canoe and catamaran rides. ⊠ *In front of Halekūlani Hotel.*

Kahaloa and Ulukou Beaches. A lot of activities and possibly the best swimming are available along this little stretch of Waikīkī Beach. Try a catamaran or outrigger canoe ride out into the bay, unless you're ready to sign up for a surfing lesson at the Waikīkī Beach Center nearby.

The Royal Hawaiian Hotel cordons off a small section of sand for its guests, bringing to mind a rich kid's sandbox. Facilities include public rest rooms, changing rooms, showers, and a snack stand. The police station is here as well. ⊠ *In front of Royal Hawaiian Hotel and Sheraton Moana Surfrider.*

Kūhiō Beach Park. Prince Jonah Kūhiō Kalaniana'ole, a distinguished native statesman, had his home here on Waikīkī's shore earlier in this century. The residence was torn down in 1950, 14 years after his death, to enlarge the beach. There's a breakwater seawall that runs out about 1,300 ft parallel to the beach from Kapahulu Groin, a cemented-over storm drain jutting out from shore at the Diamond Head end of the beach. This seawall, built to stem beach erosion, created two semi-enclosed pools, with water fairly deep out near the breakwater. Though the water appears calm, swimming here has its dangers: Unpredictably deep holes can form in the sandy bottom as a result of swirling currents, and children should be watched closely. Beyond the Groin's cement wall, boogie boarders and bodysurfers enthusiastically ride the waves. The Groin is a great place to watch a Hawaiian sunset, but be sure of your footing: It's slippery when wet. ⊠ *Waikīkī Beach Center to Kapahulu Groin.*

Queen's Surf. A great place for a sunset picnic, this beach is beyond the seawall, toward Diamond Head, at what's known as the "other end of Waikīkī." It was once the site of Queen Lili'uokalani's beach house, hence the name. A mix of families and gays gathers here, and it seems as if someone is always playing a bongo drum. There are good shade trees, picnic tables, and a changing house with showers. ⊠ *Across from entrance to Honolulu Zoo.*

Sans Souci. Nicknamed "Dig-Me Beach" because of its outlandish display of skimpy bathing suits, this small rectangle of sand is nonetheless a good sunning spot for all ages. Children enjoy its shallow, safe waters, and the shore draws many ocean kayakers and outrigger canoers. Serious swimmers and triathletes also swim in the channel here, beyond the reef. There's no food concession, but near one end is the Hau Tree Lānai, an open-air eatery that is part of the New Otani Kaimana Beach Hotel. A grassy area is popular with picnickers and volleyball buffs, and there's an outdoor shower. ⊠ *Makai side of Kapiʻolani Park, between New Otani Kaimana Beach Hotel and Waikīkī War Memorial Natatorium.*

Beaches Near Honolulu and Around the East Oaʻhu Ring

Here are some of Oʻahu's finer beaches, listed in alphabetical order.

Ala Moana Beach Park. Ala Moana has a protective reef, which keeps the waters calm and perfect for swimming. After Waikīkī, this is the most popular beach among visitors. To the Waikīkī side is a peninsula called Magic Island, with picnic tables, shady trees, and paved sidewalks ideal for jogging. Ala Moana also has playing fields, changing houses, indoor and outdoor showers, lifeguards, concession stands, and tennis courts—a beach for everyone, but only in the daytime; crimes have occurred here after dark. ⊠ *Honolulu, makai side of Ala Moana Shopping Center and Ala Moana Blvd., from Waikīkī take Bus 8 to shopping center and cross Ala Moana Blvd.*

Bellows Beach. The waves here are great for bodysurfing, and the sand is soft for sunbathing. Locals come here for the fine swimming on weekends (and holidays), when the Air Force opens the beach to civilians. There are showers, abundant parking, and plenty of spots for picnicking underneath shady ironwood trees. There is no food concession, but McDonald's and other take-out fare is available right outside the entrance gate. ⊠ *Entrance on Kalanianaʻole Hwy. near Waimānalo town center, signs on makai side of road.*

Hanauma Bay. The main attraction here is snorkeling. The coral reefs are clearly visible through the turquoise waters of this sunken crater, a designated marine preserve. Crowds flock to its palm-fringed shores and fill the water and the narrow crescent of packed sand. Beyond the reef is a popular site for scuba-diving classes. The bay is best early in the morning (7 AM), before the crowds arrive; it can be difficult to park later in the day. There is a busy food and snorkel equipment rental concession on the beach, plus changing rooms and showers. No smoking is allowed on the beach. **Hanauma Bay Snorkeling Excursions**

(☎ 808/951–1111) run to and from Waikīkī. ✉ *7455 Kala-niana'ole Hwy.,* ☎ *808/396–4229.* 🎫 *Donation $3; parking $1; mask, snorkel, and fins rental $6.* 🕙 *Thurs.–Tues. 6* AM*–7* PM*, Wed. noon–7.*

Kailua Beach Park. Steady breezes attract windsurfers by the dozens to this long, palm-fringed beach with gently sloping sands. You can rent equipment in Kailua and try it yourself. Young athletes and members of the military enjoy this beach, as do local families, so it gets pretty crowded on weekends. There are showers, changing rooms, picnic areas, and a concession stand. Buy your picnic provisions at the Kalapawai Market nearby. ✉ *Windward side, makai of Kailua town, turn right on Kailua Rd. at market, cross bridge, then turn left into beach parking lot.*

Kualoa Regional Park. This is one of the island's most beautiful picnic, camping, and beach areas. Grassy expanses border a long, narrow stretch of beach with spectacular views of Kāne'ohe Bay and the Ko'olau Mountains. Dominating the view is an islet called Mokoli'i, which rises 206 ft above the water. At low tide you can wade out to the island on the reef, but be sure to wear sneakers. The one drawback is that it's usually windy. Bring a cooler; no refreshments are sold here. There are places to shower, change, and picnic in the shade of palm trees. ✉ *Windward side, makai of Kamehameha Hwy., north of Waiāhole.*

Makapu'u Beach. Swimming at Makapu'u should be attempted only by strong strokers and bodysurfers, because the swells can be overwhelmingly big and powerful. Instead, consider this tiny crescent cove—popular with the locals— as a prime sunbathing spot. The beach lies at the base of high cliffs: Look up, and you just might see a hang glider being launched from the bluffs overhead. With its small lot, parking can be tricky here. In a pinch, try parking on the narrow shoulder and walking down to the beach. There is a changing house with indoor and outdoor showers. ✉ *Makai of Kalaniana'ole Hwy., across from Sea Life Park, 2 mi south of Waimānalo.*

Sandy Beach. Strong, steady winds make "Sandy's" a kite-flyer's paradise. But the shore break is vicious here, and there's generally a rescue truck parked on the road, which means that people are swimming where they shouldn't and getting hurt. Do not swim here. Sandy's is a popular spot for the high school and college crowd. There's a changing house with indoor and outdoor showers, but no food concessions. ⊠ *Makai of Kalaniana'ole Hwy., 2 mi east of Hanauma Bay.*

Sunset Beach. This is another link in the chain of North Shore beaches, which extends for miles. It is popular for its gentle summer waves and crashing winter surf. The beach is broad, and the sand is soft. Lining the adjacent highway there are usually carry-out truck stands selling shave ice, plate lunches, and sodas. A new comfort station with showers, rest rooms, and a paved parking lot was expected to open on the mauka side of the highway in late 1998. ⊠ *North shore, 1 mi north of 'Ehukai Beach Park, on makai side of Kamehameha Hwy.*

Waimānalo Beach Park. Boogie-boarders and bodysurfers enjoy the predictably gentle waves of this beach. The lawn at Waimānalo attracts hundreds of local people who set up minicamps for the weekend, complete with hibachis, radios, lawn chairs, coolers, and shade tarps. Sometimes these folks are not very friendly to tourists, but the beach itself is more welcoming, and from here you can walk a mile along the shore for fantastic windward and mountain views. The grassy, shady grounds have picnic tables and shower houses. ⊠ *Windward side, look for signs makai of Kalaniana'ole Hwy., south of Waimānalo town.*

7 Shopping

AS THE CAPITAL OF THE 50TH STATE, Honolulu is the number-one shopping town in the Islands and an international crossroads of the shopping scene. It has sprawling shopping malls, spiffy boutiques, hotel stores, family-run businesses, and a variety of other enterprises selling brand-new merchandise as well as priceless antiques and one-of-a-kind souvenirs and gifts. As you drive around the island, you'll find souvenir stands and what appear to be discount stores for local products; merchandise here is often tacky and expensive.

Updated by Marty Wentzel

Major shopping malls are generally open daily from 10 to 9, although some shops may close at 4 or 5.

Shopping Centers

In Waikīkī

The fashionable new **King Kalākaua Plaza** (✉ 2080 Kalākaua Ave.) opened its flagship store **Banana Republic** in late 1997, with **NikeTown, All Star Cafe**, and other high-profile tenants opening throughout 1998.

Royal Hawaiian Shopping Center (✉ 2201 Kalākaua Ave., ☎ 808/922–0588 for information on free hula lessons, crafts demonstrations, and other special events), fronting the Royal Hawaiian and Sheraton Waikīkī hotels, is three blocks long and contains 120 stores on three levels. There are such upscale establishments as **Chanel** and **Cartier,** as well as local arts and crafts from the **Little Hawaiian Craft Shop,** which features Bishop Museum reproductions, Ni'ihau shell leis (those super-expensive leis from the island of Ni'ihau), feather hatbands, and South Pacific art. **Bijoux Jewelers** has a fun collection of baubles, bangles, and beads for your perusal. **Royal Hawaiian Gems** fashions gold bracelets, necklaces, and rings with Hawaiian names engraved in them. You can get a refreshing shave ice at **Island Snow Hawai'i** and buy a whimsical T-shirt at **Crazy Shirts Hawai'i.**

Waikīkī Shopping Plaza (✉ 2270 Kalākaua Ave.) is across the street from the Royal Hawaiian Shopping Center. Its landmark is a 75-ft-high water-sculpture gizmo, which looks great when it's working. **Sawada Pro Golf Shop** sells accessories to improve your game.

Waikīkī Trade Center (⊠ At the corner of Kūhiō and Seaside Aves.) is slightly out of the action and has shops only on the first floor. **Bebe Sport,** which leans to the leather look, is for the slim and affluent. **C. June Shoes** offers European designer shoes, clothing, handbags, belts, and accessories. Need some water sportswear? Stop by the **Town & Country Surf Shop.**

Waikīkī has three theme-park-style shopping centers. Right in the heart of the area is the **International Market Place** (⊠ 2330 Kalākaua Ave.), a tangle of 200 souvenir shops and stalls under a giant banyan tree. **Waikīkī Town Center** (⊠ 2301 Kūhiō Ave.) has plenty of touristy beads, beach towels, and shirts. **King's Village** (⊠ 131 Ka'iulani Ave., ☎ 808/944–6855 for special-event information) looks like a Hollywood stage set of monarchy-era Honolulu, complete with a changing-of-the-guard ceremony every evening at 6:15.

Around Honolulu

Ala Moana Shopping Center (⊠ 1450 Ala Moana Blvd., ☎ 808/946–2811 for special-event information) is a gigantic open-air mall just five minutes from Waikīkī by bus. The 50-acre, 200-shop center is on the corner of Atkinson and Ala Moana boulevards. All of Hawai'i's major department stores are here, including **Neiman Marcus, Nordstrom, Sears,** and **JCPenney. Liberty House** is highly recommended for its selection of stylish Hawaiian wear. Upscale fashions are available at **Gucci, Ann Taylor, Chanel, Louis Vuitton,** and **Emporio Armani.** For stunning Hawaiian prints, try the **Art Board,** and buy your local footwear at the **Slipper House.**

Ala Moana also has a huge assortment of local-style souvenir shops, such as **Hawaiian Island Creations, Irene's Hawaiian Gifts,** and **Products of Hawai'i.** Its **Makai Market** is a large international food bazaar. Stores at Ala Moana open their doors daily at 9:30 AM. The shopping center closes Monday through Saturday at 9 PM and Sunday at 5, with longer hours during the Christmas holidays.

Heading west from Waikīkī, toward downtown Honolulu, you'll run into **Ward Warehouse** (⊠ 1050 Ala Moana Blvd.), a two-story mall with 65 shops and restaurants. **Ward Centre** (⊠ 1200 Ala Moana Blvd.) has 30 upscale boutiques and eateries, including **R. Field Wine Co.** and **Compadres** (Mexican food).

Restaurant Row (⊠ 500 Ala Moana Blvd. between South and Punchbowl Sts., ☎ 808/538–1441 for special-event information) is a trendy conglomeration of fun retailers and eateries. Stop by **Honolulu Chocolate Company** for the best sweets this side of Paradise.

Aloha Tower Marketplace (⊠ 101 Ala Moana Blvd., at Piers 8, 9, and 10, ☎ 808/528–5700 for special-event information) cozies up to Honolulu Harbor and bills itself as a festival marketplace. Along with restaurants and entertainment venues, it has shops and kiosks selling mostly visitor-oriented merchandise, from expensive sunglasses to souvenir refrigerator magnets.

Aloha Flea Market is a thrice-weekly outdoor bazaar that attracts hundreds of merchants and thousands of bargain hunters. Operations range from slick tents with rows of neatly stacked, new wares to blankets spread on the pavement, covered with rusty tools and cracked china. You'll find gold trinkets, antique furniture, digital watches, Japanese fishing floats, T-shirts, muʻumuʻu, and palm-frond hats. Price haggling—in moderation—is the order of the day. ⊠ *99-500 Salt Lake Blvd.,* ☎ *808/732–9611.* ⊡ *$6, including round-trip shuttle from Waikīkī.* ⊙ *Wed. and weekends 6–3.*

Kāhala Mall (⊠ 4211 Waiʻalae Ave.) is 10 minutes by car from Waikīkī in the chic residential neighborhood of Kāhala, near the slopes of Diamond Head. This mall features such clothing stores as **Liberty House** and **The Gap. Reyn's** is the acknowledged place to go for men's resort wear; its aloha shirts have muted colors and button-down collars, suitable for most social occasions. **Banana Republic** has outdoor wear. Along with an assortment of gift shops, Kāhala Mall also has **eight movie theaters** (☎ 808/733–6233) for post-shopping entertainment.

The **Waikele Shopping Plaza** (⊠ H-1 Fwy., 10 min west of downtown Honolulu) reflects Hawai'i's latest craze: warehouse shopping at discount prices. Among its occupants is the **Sports Authority**.

Specialty Stores

Clothing

HIGH FASHION

Chocolates for Breakfast (⊠ Ala Moana Shopping Center, ☎ 808/947–3434) is the trendy end of the high-fashion scene. For the latest in shoes and bags, **C. June Shoes** (⊠ Waikīkī Trade Center, ☎ 808/926–1574) displays an elegant array of pricey styles. Top-of-the-line international fashions for men and women are available at **Mandalay Imports** (⊠ Halekūlani, 2199 Kālia Rd., ☎ 808/922–7766), home of Star of Siam silks and cottons, Anne Namba couture, and designs by Choisy, who works out of Bangkok. **Pzazz** (⊠ 1419 Kalākaua Ave., ☎ 808/955–5800), which sells high fashion at low prices, is nicknamed the Ann Taylor of consignment shops.

RESORT WEAR

For stylish Hawaiian wear, the kind worn by local men and women, look in one of the **Liberty House** branches at Ala Moana Shopping Center, Kāhala Mall (☞ Shopping Centers, *above*), or in downtown Honolulu (⊠ 2314 Kalākaua Ave., Waikīkī, ☎ 808/941–2345 for all stores). **Carol & Mary** (⊠ Halekūlani, ☎ 808/971–4269; ⊠ Hilton Hawaiian Village, ☎ 808/973–5395; ⊠ Royal Hawaiian Hotel, ☎ 808/971–4262) sells high-end resort wear for women. Moderately priced mu'umu'u may be found at **Andrade** (⊠ Sheraton Princess Ka'iulani Hotel, ☎ 808/971–4266; ⊠ Sheraton Waikīkī Hotel, ☎ 808/971–4264). For menswear, try **Reyn's** (⊠ Ala Moana Shopping Center, ☎ 808/949–5929; ⊠ Kāhala Mall, ☎ 808/737–8313; ⊠ Sheraton Waikīkī Hotel, ☎ 808/923–0331).

If you want something bright, bold, and cheap, try **Hilo Hattie** (⊠ 700 N. Nimitz Hwy., ☎ 808/544–3500), the world's largest manufacturer of Hawaiian and tropical fashions. For convenience, they offer free shuttle service from Waikīkī. For vintage aloha shirts, try **Bailey's Antique Clothing and**

Thrift Shop (⊠ 517 Kapahulu Ave., ☎ 808/734–7628), on the edge of Waikīkī.

McInerny has several locations (⊠ Ala Moana Shopping Center, ☎ 808/973–5380; ⊠ Hilton Hawaiian Village, ☎ 808/973–5392; ⊠ Royal Hawaiian Hotel, ☎ 808/971–4263; ⊠ Royal Hawaiian Shopping Center, ☎ 808/971–4275) where you can find a wide selection of colorful resort wear for men and women, with styles for day and evening.

Food

Bring home some fresh pineapple, papaya, or coconut to savor or share with your friends and family. Jam comes in flavors like pohā, passion fruit, and guava. Kona coffee has an international following. There are such dried-food products as saimin, *haupia* (a firm coconut pudding), and teriyaki barbecue sauce. All kinds of cookies are available, as well as exotic teas, drink mixes, and pancake syrups. And don't forget the macadamia nuts, from plain to chocolate-covered and brittled. By law, all fresh-fruit products must be inspected by the Department of Agriculture. The stores listed below carry only inspected fruit, ready for shipment. For cheap prices on local delicacies, try one of the many **Long's Drugs** stores (⊠ Ala Moana Shopping Center, 1450 Ala Moana Blvd., 2nd level, ☎ 808/941–4433; Kāhala Mall, ☎ 808/732–0784; ⊠ 1088 Bishop Street Mall, downtown, ☎ 808/536–4551). **Tropical Fruits Distributors of Hawai'i** (⊠ 64-1551 Kamehameha Hwy., Honolulu, ☎ 808/621–7062) specializes in packing inspected pineapple and papaya; they will deliver to your hotel and to the airport baggage check-in counter or ship to the mainland United States and Canada.

Gifts

Robyn Buntin Galleries (⊠ 848 S. Beretania St., Honolulu, ☎ 808/523–5913) presents Chinese nephrite jade carvings, Japanese lacquer and screens, Buddhist sculptures, and other international pieces. **Takenoya Arts** (⊠ Halekūlani, 2199 Kālia Rd., ☎ 808/926–1939) specializes in intricately carved *netsuke* (toggles used to fasten containers to kimonos), both antique and contemporary, and one-of-a-kind necklaces. **Following Sea** (⊠ Kāhala Mall, ☎ 808/734–4425) sells beautiful handmade jewelry and pottery.

Hawaiian Art and Crafts

One of the nicest gifts is something handcrafted of native Hawaiian wood. Some species of trees grow only in Hawai'i. Koa and milo each have a beautiful color and grain. The great koa forests are disappearing because of environmental factors, so the wood is becoming valuable.

The best selection of Hawaiian arts and crafts in Waikīkī is at the **Little Hawaiian Craft Shop** (⊠ Royal Hawaiian Shopping Center, ☎ 808/926–2662). Some items are Bishop Museum reproductions, with a portion of the profits going to the museum. The shop also has a good selection of Ni'ihau shell leis, feather hatbands, and South Pacific arts.

For hula costumes and instruments, try **Hula Supply Center** (⊠ 2346 S. King St., ☎ 808/941–5379). For comforters stitched with traditional Island designs, try **Quilts Hawai'i** (⊠ 2338 S. King St., ☎ 808/942–3195). For high-end collector's items, head to **Martin & MacArthur** (⊠ Aloha Tower Marketplace, ☎ 808/524–6066), specialists in koa furniture.

Jewelry

You can buy gold chains by the inch on the street corner, and jade and coral trinkets by the dozen. **Bernard Hurtig's** (⊠ Hilton Hawaiian Village Ali'i Tower, ☎ 808/947–9399; ⊠ Tapa Tower, ☎ 808/955–3559) has fine jewelry with an emphasis on 18-karat gold and antique jade. Hawaiian heirloom jewelry is popular with Island residents. Bracelets, earrings, and necklaces are imprinted with distinctive black letters that spell out your name in Hawaiian. In Waikīkī, try **Royal Hawaiian Heritage Jewelry** (⊠ 4325 Seaside Ave., ☎ 808/922–9699; ⊠ 1525 Kalākaua Ave., ☎ 808/942–7474).

Haimoff & Haimoff Creations in Gold (⊠ Halekūlani, 2199 Kālia Rd., ☎ 808/923–8777) sells the original work of award-winning jewelry designer Harry Haimoff.

INDEX

✕ = *restaurant*, 🏠 = *hotel*

WHEREVER YOU TRAVEL, 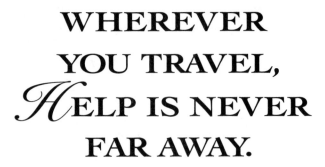ELP IS NEVER FAR AWAY.

From planning your trip to providing travel assistance along the way, American Express® Travel Service Offices are always there to help you do more.

Honolulu & Waikiki

Commerce Tower, Suite 104
1440 Kapiolani Blvd.
808/946-7741

Hilton Hawaiian Village
2005 Kalia Road
808/947-2607

Hyatt Regency Waikiki
2424 Kalakaua Avenue
808/926-5441/TFS: 922-4718

do more AMERICAN EXPRESS®

Travel
www.americanexpress.com/travel

American Express Travel Service Offices are located throughout Hawaii. For the office nearest you, call 1-800-AXP-3429.

Listings are valid as of September 1998. Not all services available at all locations.
© 1998 American Express.